PAY OR FIGHT?

THE TRUTH ABOUT MAINTENANCE LAWS IN INDIA

OVER 1000+ COPIES OF E-BOOKS SOLD

NITISH BANKA (ADVOCATE)

BlueRose ONE.com
Stories Matter
NewDelhi • London

BLUEROSE PUBLISHERS
India | U.K.

BlueRose ONE
Stories Matter
NewDelhi • London

For permissions requests or inquiries regarding this publication, please contact:

BLUEROSE PUBLISHERS
www.BlueRoseONE.com
info@bluerosepublishers.com
+91 8882 898 898
+4407342408967

ISBN: 978-93-7139-277-8

Cover Design: Shubham Verma
Typesetting: Sagar

First Edition: September 2025

Nitish Banka

Advocate, Supreme court of India, Delhi | Founder, Lexspeak Legal

Nitish Banka is a distinguished advocate with over a decade of experience in matrimonial and maintenance law. He has successfully represented clients before Family Courts, High Courts across India, and the Hon'ble Supreme Court, handling complex and emotionally sensitive matters involving maintenance, domestic violence, child custody, and false 498A allegations. His legal acumen extends across various statutory frameworks including Section 125 CrPC, the Domestic Violence Act, and the Hindu Marriage Act. He is known for his ability to design courtroom strategies that cut through vague and generalized allegations, uncover the truth behind inflated claims, and protect the legal and financial interests of his clients.

As the founder of Lexspeak Legal, Nitish has built one of the most trusted legal platforms in India for individuals facing matrimonial disputes. His mission has been to simplify the law for those who need it the most. Through his widely followed YouTube channel "Lexspeak Legal," which has over 160,000 subscribers, he has educated thousands of people by breaking down complicated legal procedures into practical and actionable guidance. His videos on maintenance law, child custody, and misuse of legal provisions such as 498A have empowered litigants across the country to approach the courts with confidence and clarity.

Nitish Banka's legal practice spans across the country. He has argued and secured favorable judgments in High Courts including those in Delhi, Bombay, Calcutta, Karnataka, Allahabad, Uttarakhand, Punjab and Haryana, Patna, Rajasthan, Madhya Pradesh, and others. His pan-India presence and vast experience give him a unique perspective on how different High Courts interpret maintenance-related provisions, making him a go-to counsel for clients looking for strategic representation in complex cases. His deep understanding of evolving judicial trends and procedural nuances, including recent developments under the Bharatiya Nyaya Sanhita, allows him to stay ahead of the curve and deliver results.

This book is the culmination of Nitish's years of practical experience in handling real-world matrimonial disputes. It serves as both a legal guide and a practical companion for anyone navigating the challenging terrain of maintenance litigation be it a husband fighting an unjust claim, a wife seeking rightful support, a lawyer looking for strong legal arguments, or a family dealing with the emotional and financial impact of a separation. With this book, Nitish hopes to bring clarity to confusion, strength to struggle, and a structured legal path to those caught in the web of maintenance litigation.

Driven by a belief that clarity, strategy, and inner strength are the pillars of justice in family law matters, Nitish Banka continues to dedicate his work to ensuring that litigants are not just legally represented, but truly heard and empowered throughout their legal journey.

Author's Note on Legal Provisions Referenced in This Book

The legal provisions, sections, and references made throughout this book are based on the older criminal laws of India, specifically the Code of Criminal Procedure, 1973 (CrPC), the Indian Penal Code, 1860 (IPC), and the Indian Evidence Act, 1872. These laws formed the basis of the Indian criminal justice system for decades and continue to govern a large body of judicial precedents related to matrimonial and maintenance matters.

This book does not cover or interpret the newly enacted criminal law codes, namely:

- Bharatiya Nyaya Sanhita, 2023 (BNS), which replaces the Indian Penal Code
- Bharatiya Nagarik Suraksha Sanhita, 2023 (BNSS), which replaces the Code of Criminal Procedure
- Bharatiya Sakshya Adhiniyam, 2023 (BSA), which replaces the Indian Evidence Act

The reason for relying exclusively on the older legal framework is that the vast majority of case law, practical experience, and strategic insights related to maintenance laws are grounded in these statutes. The new codes, although enacted, are relatively recent, and the legal community is still in the process of interpreting and applying them. At the time of writing this book, most courts continue to refer to and rely on the earlier statutes for adjudicating maintenance cases.

I request readers' understanding and cooperation in this regard. This book is intended to be a practical and strategic guide based on well-established legal processes and precedents. Future editions may address the impact of the new laws once a stable body of jurisprudence emerges under the updated legal framework.

— Author

Why I Felt Compelled to Write This Book on Maintenance — and How to Strategically Reduce It

It all started with a call I received one late evening from a distraught man named Ramesh (name changed for privacy). He was in his early 30s, an IT professional, and sounded utterly defeated. His voice trembled as he explained how a maintenance order from the family court had just been passed against himan amount he could scarcely afford even after stretching every rupee of his monthly salary. “Sir,” he said, “I don’t mind supporting her reasonably, but how can I survive if most of my salary is going to her while I live like a pauper?” His family, especially his aging parents who were financially dependent on him, were equally shaken.

That wasn't the first call I received of this nature, and it certainly wouldn’t be the last.

In fact, over the years, I noticed a disturbing pattern. Husbandsmost of them ordinary middle-class professionals were being financially strangled in the name of maintenance. They were clueless, scared, and badly advised, often signing off on lopsided settlements just to get some breathing room. They were told: *"Just pay it. It's better to end it fast."* No strategy. No structured guidance. Just a vague sense of defeat.

This is where I began to feel a growing unease. As a legal practitioner, I had access to tools, precedents, and strategies that could have helped men like Ramesh. Yet, I saw that even some seasoned lawyers treated maintenance proceedings as a formality, or worse, as a procedural pit stop en route to a divorce. The very real and crushing financial impact was not being addressed with the seriousness it deserved.

In most matrimonial disputes, especially those entangled in allegations and counter-allegations, ***maintenance becomes the single most burdensome sword hanging over the husband's head***. It is not uncommon for maintenance proceedings to become the leverage tool used to push for inflated settlements. The law, as it stands, leans heavily in favor of the wife often without factoring in the ground realities of the husband's financial obligations or standard of living. The presumption of need is almost automatic, and in the rush of hearings, pleadings, and affidavits, the nuances of fairness are often lost.

I recall another case where a husband, having won most arguments on the merits of the case, still had to pay a staggering amount in interim maintenance. "Why bother fighting the main case if I'm already bleeding financially?" he asked. He had a point. The sheer weight of ongoing maintenance payments can force even the strongest litigants into submission.

Through all these cases, I realized a simple truth: *maintenance is not just a legal issue; it's a strategy issue.* And like any good strategy, it needs planning, understanding, and execution.

This book is the result of that realization.

It is written for husbands who find themselves blindsided by maintenance claims. It is for the families who want to support them but don't know how. And, frankly, it is for legal professionals who need to start treating maintenance strategy as a vital part of the overall litigation roadmap.

This book will walk you through the legal framework, yes—but more importantly, it will arm you with practical tactics, real case insights, and strategic decisions that can help reduce or even eliminate unfair maintenance claims. Because unless maintenance is controlled early in the proceedings, it leaves little room for a fair settlement later. And that's what every party in a matrimonial dispute ultimately seeks a resolution that is just, balanced, and sustainable.

So, if you are facing a maintenance battle, know this: you are not alone, and with the right strategy, you are not powerless either.

Now, maintenance law is quite simple: if the wife is not earning, the husband must pay maintenance, regardless of whether the wife left the marital home voluntarily. Even in cases of cheating or extramarital affairs, the husband is still liable to pay maintenance. While maintenance cases may not seem harmful initially, issues arise at the interim stage when maintenance is decided, which could be one or two years after the case is filed.

According to the new guidelines of the honorable Supreme Court, the husband must pay maintenance from the date of the petition being filing. This means the husband may owe a significant sum in arrears, which can run into lakhs of rupees, to the wife as soon as the maintenance procedure begins.

Failure to pay maintenance can result in execution proceedings, which may lead to serious consequences such as imprisonment or attachment of the husband's movable or immovable properties, including salary or bank accounts, as directed by the court. This enforcement mechanism is often the most feared aspect for husbands embroiled in matrimonial disputes. The threat of arrest or financial seizure adds immense pressure, especially when these proceedings run parallel to protracted and emotionally draining divorce cases that often yield no conclusive outcome for years. The combination of indefinite litigation and stringent enforcement of maintenance orders can create a situation of prolonged legal and financial vulnerability for husbands.

The book I've written is not just a legal commentary it's a guide born out of real struggles faced by countless husbands caught in the relentless grip of maintenance litigation. Over the years, I've seen men walk into my office, shoulders heavy with the burden of financial obligations they could barely meet, fearing arrest or asset seizure. Some had already faced execution proceedings, their salaries garnished or properties attached, while their divorce cases dragged on without resolution.

This book aims to provide a ray of hope in such overwhelming circumstances not by offering false promises, but by sharing practical, time-tested strategies that can lead to significant relief, and in some cases, even reduce maintenance to zero. Yes, that's possible—but only when the facts, timing, and approach align correctly. I've personally been involved in numerous cases where we've managed to substantially reduce maintenance through careful planning, sharp legal reasoning, and well-timed negotiation during divorce proceedings.

That said, every case is different. One of the most important lessons I've learned is the value of honesty with clients not every situation allows for reduction, and giving false hope only worsens the emotional and financial toll. Still, even when reduction isn't viable, alternative strategies can be deployed. Whether it's contesting jurisdiction, challenging the wife's claims with solid evidence, or navigating procedural nuances to build pressure for a fair settlement there is always a way to shift the balance.

This book brings together those techniques, insights, and practical tools. It's not about avoiding responsibility, but about seeking fairness and protecting oneself in a system that often feels one-sided. Through each chapter, my goal is to equip husbands with knowledge not just legal, but strategic so they can walk into courtrooms prepared, not defeated.

Contents

Chapter-1
"Why Maintenance Feels Like a Trap:
The Silent Struggle of Husbands" 1

Chapter 2
How Much Is Too Much? Understanding
The Real Cost of Maintenance 11

Chapter 3
Inside The Courtroom: Step-By-Step Breakdown
of Maintenance Cases 18

Chapter 4
What The Judge Sees: How Maintenance Amounts
Are Decided 30

Chapter 5
Unmasking The Hidden Income:
The Art of Evidence Discovery 41

Chapter 6
What Really Counts: Expenses That Can Make
or Break Your Case 49

Chapter 7
Zero Rupee Game: Strategies To Eliminate or Slash Maintenance 56

Chapter 8
Cross-Border Maintenance: Fighting Fair When You're a Nri 64

Chapter 9
The Endgame: Negotiating Smart Settlements & Closing the Case 73

Chapter 10
Evolution of Maintenance Jurisprudence in India: From *Rupali Gupta v. Rajat Gupta* to *Rajnesh v. Neha* 81

Chapter 11
The Landmark of Maintenance Laws : Rajnesh v. Neha 89

Chapter-1

"Why Maintenance Feels Like a Trap: The Silent Struggle of Husbands"

Maintenance law — a term that appears straightforward in textbooks — unfolds into a labyrinthine struggle in the real world, particularly for husbands entangled in matrimonial disputes. It begins with a petition or complaint, but soon spirals into a prolonged financial and emotional battle. As a practicing lawyer, I've seen this time and again: maintenance is not merely a legal obligation, it's a pressure tactic that can break a man long before the court delivers justice.

It begins, often, with a marriage filled with promises. A man and a woman step into what they believe is a lifelong bond, committing to support each other through life's uncertainties. But when the relationship breaks down and separation becomes inevitable, the emotional wounds are only the beginning. For many husbands in India, what follows is a slow and silent descent into a legal maze that feels more like a trap than a path to justice.

The law of maintenance, as it stands today, was designed with noble intentions. It seeks to prevent destitution. It aims to ensure that a financially dependent spouse traditionally the wife does not suffer after separation. But in practice, maintenance has often become a powerful tool of pressure, and in some cases, misuse. For thousands of men across India, especially those caught in long-drawn-out litigation, the law doesn't feel like protection it feels like punishment.

A Case that Shook the Community

Consider the tragic story of *Amit Bansal* (name changed), a 38-year-old software engineer in Noida. In 2023, after his wife filed for maintenance under multiple provisions, he was ordered to pay ₹50,000 per month—nearly 60% of his take-home salary. The court order also made him liable for arrears going back over two years, amounting to over ₹11 lakhs. Despite struggling to keep up with EMIs, rent, and parental medical expenses, Amit had no option but to comply. The court warned of execution proceedings if payments were delayed. Friends described him as a calm, family-oriented man, but as the legal pressure mounted, he began to show signs of withdrawal and depression. One day, he left a note on his desk—"I am not a criminal, just a broken man" and took his life.

His story is not an isolated one. Across metros and small towns alike, there have been numerous cases in recent years of men pushed to the brink some into debt, some into despair, some into silence. A man in Bengaluru was jailed for defaulting on maintenance even though he had lost his job during the pandemic. Another in Punjab reportedly sold his car, withdrew his provident fund, and borrowed money just to avoid arrest due to unpaid interim maintenance. In some cases, elderly parents of these men are forced to shoulder financial burdens they never imagined.

Why It Feels Like a Trap

Unlike other forms of litigation, maintenance proceedings begin with an assumption of obligation. The wife claims she is dependent, and the husband is immediately put in the spotlight. He must prove what he earns, what he spends, what he owns and justify every rupee. But the wife's financial disclosures are often taken lightly. Her ability to earn, past employment, or present income is rarely scrutinized with the same intensity.

Interim maintenance is routinely granted on the first or second hearing, sometimes ex parte, based solely on the wife's version. Arrears are calculated from the date of the petition, not the date of the order, as per the ***Rajnesh v. Neha*** judgment. This means a man who is trying to navigate a divorce, possibly facing false allegations or custody battles, may also be handed a crushing financial liability dating back months or even years.

There is little scope to argue affordability at the interim stage. Even if the husband loses his job or suffers losses in business, the courts often expect continuity in payment. In some cases, even borrowing or selling assets is considered a "reasonable expectation" for compliance.

Failure to pay is not treated as an economic limitation but as wilful disobedience punishable with attachment of property or imprisonment.

The Unseen Emotional Toll

Most men do not talk about this. There are no public protests, no media panels discussing the psychological burden of maintenance litigation. But in legal chambers, court corridors, and counselling centres, you hear the stories the fear of losing one's freedom, the pain of being painted as a negligent husband, the helplessness of watching parents sell jewellery to pay maintenance.

The emotional toll is staggering. Men who once held respectable jobs are reduced to explaining themselves to strangers in courtrooms. Fathers who long to see their children are instead cross-examined about every financial decision. The system treats them not as individuals in crisis, but as walking wallets. This emotional suppression leads to stress disorders, breakdowns, substance abuse, and tragically, in some cases, suicide.

The Cost to Society

What is perhaps less discussed is the broader cost to Indian society morally, ethically, and economically. A society thrives when justice is balanced and equitable. But when laws are misapplied or perceived as one-sided, they erode trust. Men begin to fear marriage. Families discourage their sons from marrying without legal safeguards. Some choose not to marry at all, worried about the consequences of a breakdown.

This fear has larger consequences. The institution of marriage itself is now viewed by many urban men with suspicion. As maintenance claims grow in number and severity, the idea of partnership is replaced by caution and contracts. This erodes the emotional foundation on which families are built.

Economically, prolonged litigation drains not just the individuals involved, but also the judicial system. Cases drag on for years, clogging family courts. Legal fees mount. Resources are spent not on rehabilitation or reconciliation, but on enforcement and execution. Meanwhile, genuine victims wives who truly need support also suffer due to the backlog and delays caused by the sheer volume of contested or inflated claims.

The Moral Dilemma

There is also a deeper moral dilemma. Maintenance law was created to protect the vulnerable, not to weaponize dependency. But when a qualified, educated, and capable individual chooses to remain unemployed just to continue drawing maintenance, it challenges the ethical core of the law. When husbands are stripped of dignity, labelled defaulters, or jailed without assessing their genuine financial situation, it questions the humaneness of the process.

Justice must be compassionate but not blind. A one-size-fits-all approach to maintenance fails both men and women. It rewards silence over truth, compliance over fairness, and creates a culture where legal battles are waged not for justice, but for advantage.

A Call for Fairness

This book does not seek to vilify maintenance law. The right to maintenance is a legitimate and necessary safeguard. But what it demands is balance. Husbands, too, deserve fairness, compassion, and the benefit of doubt. They deserve to be heard not just in courtrooms, but in the national conversation.

We must begin to see maintenance not just as a legal concept, but as a social reality with far reaching consequences. It's time to acknowledge that men, too, can be victims not of gender, but of a system that sometimes forgets that justice must have two eyes, not one.

This chapter is not just an argument; it is a voice. A voice for those who feel trapped but cannot speak. A voice for the men who walk into court not to evade responsibility, but to seek dignity.

And above all, it is a reminder that true justice lies not in punishment, but in balance.

Why did I feel the need to write this book? The answer is simple — because most husbands walk into litigation unarmed. They are unaware of their rights, of the procedures, of the ways to challenge or even reduce the maintenance demanded. They either overpay out of fear or drag themselves through years of litigation that leaves them drained financially, emotionally, and psychologically.

Maintenance law, while rooted in the intention of safeguarding dependents, has evolved into a one-sided battlefield in many cases. The moment a husband faces a maintenance case whether under Section 125 CrPC, the Domestic Violence Act, or the Hindu Marriage Act he is often presumed guilty. He must pay, no matter the circumstances. Did the wife leave voluntarily? Was there cruelty from her side? Is she capable of earning? None of that matters in the early stages. Interim maintenance gets slapped on often without deep scrutiny and from that point onward, the husband begins to feel the trap tighten.

Even more troubling is the arrears concept. Following the Rajnesh vs Neha judgment, interim maintenance is calculated from the date of the petition – not the date of order. So by the time an order comes through, the husband might already owe lakhs in arrears. Miss a few payments, and he faces execution proceedings, which could mean jail time, salary attachment, or property seizure. Imagine battling a drawn-out divorce case, already weighing down your life, and now facing possible imprisonment simply because the court assumed your financial standing based on incomplete or misleading affidavits.

This book is born from my hands-on experience with such cases. I've helped countless clients reduce their maintenance obligations, some even to zero but always with realistic expectations and lawful strategies. It's not about evading responsibilities. It's about asserting fairness in a system that often overlooks the husband's side of the story.

Here, you will learn not just the legal procedures but also the practical strategies: how to call for hidden documents, how to contest inflated claims, how to present your true financial standing, and most importantly, when to fight and when to settle. Because fighting blindly can sometimes cost more than settling smartly.

Let's be honest men don't talk about this enough. Maintenance proceedings are emotionally taxing, and the social stigma of a man asking for fairness in a wife-centric law often prevents many from even seeking help. This book is for them the silent strugglers who've been pushed into the shadows of matrimonial litigation.

This is not a manual filled with empty promises. It is a toolkit – built on law, logic, and lived experiences for those who are ready to fight smart.

The Emotional Toll of Maintenance Cases

Maintenance disputes often leave husbands emotionally drained. Beyond the financial burden, many men face the stress of constant court hearings, the anxiety of wage attachments, and the looming threat of jail time. This process can feel like a slow-moving storm, disrupting not only personal finances but also mental health and family relationships. It's common for husbands to feel isolated and misunderstood, as society rarely acknowledges the emotional challenges they endure during maintenance litigation. This book is mindful of that silent struggle and aims to provide both legal clarity and emotional support through practical guidance.

The Imbalance in Legal Awareness

One of the biggest hurdles husbands face in maintenance proceedings is a lack of clear, accessible legal information. Most men find themselves navigating a confusing maze without a reliable map or guide. The law itself can be complex, and court procedures are often slow and intimidating. Without proper legal advice, husbands risk overpaying or missing key opportunities to contest inflated claims. This book bridges that gap, providing straightforward explanations and strategic advice to empower readers to take control of their cases with confidence and clarity.

Common Myths and Misconceptions

Maintenance law is surrounded by myths that often mislead husbands into thinking they have no options. Many believe that once maintenance is claimed, it cannot be challenged, or that paying maintenance is equivalent to admitting fault. Such misconceptions create unnecessary fear and resignation. In truth, the law offers multiple avenues to contest or reduce maintenance, provided the right evidence and strategies are used. Early in this book, we will debunk these myths to equip you with the facts because understanding your rights is the first step toward fairness.

Why Maintenance Law Seems One-Sided

It's no secret that maintenance laws, especially in India, have historically favored wives to ensure their financial security post-separation. This focus was necessary to protect women who lacked earning capacity or were economically dependent. However, in many cases today, the law's application can feel one-sided, leaving husbands at a disadvantage especially if the wife is capable of earning or voluntarily leaves the marital home. Fortunately, recent court rulings have begun to balance the scales by considering factors such as the wife's income, conduct, and reasons for leaving. This book will guide you through those nuances so you can present a fair case.

Setting Realistic Expectations

While this book offers strategies to reduce or eliminate maintenance, it is important to approach each case with realistic expectations. No single solution fits all situations. Some claims cannot be fully dismissed due to the facts of the case or legal constraints. At times, pursuing a fair and reasonable settlement might be the wisest path. By understanding the strengths and limitations of your case, you will be better prepared to make informed decisions rather than chasing false hopes. This book encourages smart, pragmatic approaches to protect your financial and emotional well-being.

Chapter 2

How Much Is Too Much? Understanding The Real Cost of Maintenance

One of the most urgent concerns for husbands facing maintenance proceedings is to understand the actual amount they may be required to pay. Knowing how courts arrive at maintenance figures is crucial—not only to prepare financially but also to plan effective legal strategies that could help reduce or negotiate the amount.

Maintenance amounts are not fixed; they vary widely based on several key factors, primarily the husband's income, the wife's earning capacity, and whether children are involved. Courts consider these factors carefully, but the general range and methodology have been shaped by judicial precedents and practical experience.

Situation	Maintenance Percentage
Wife not working	30% - 40% of in-hand salary or income approximately
Wife not working, with one child	50% - 60% of in-hand salary or income approximately
Wife not working, with two children	60% - 70% of in-hand salary or income approximately
Wife working Equal income	No Maintenance
Wife working but 1 Child	30% - 40% of in-hand salary or income approximately

Maintenance Without Children

In cases where the wife is not employed and there are no children, the court generally orders maintenance at about 30 to 40 percent of the husband's in-hand salary or monthly income. This proportion is meant to cover the wife's basic necessities—food, clothing, shelter, and other personal expenses—allowing her to maintain a modest standard of living.

Although 30 to 40 percent of one's salary may feel substantial, it reflects the court's intent to ensure that a financially dependent spouse does not suffer undue hardship. The law presumes that a wife who has no income should continue to live in a manner somewhat comparable to the marital standard of living.

Maintenance With Children

The financial responsibility naturally escalates once children enter the picture. The court's primary concern shifts to safeguarding the welfare of the children, alongside ensuring the wife's maintenance.

For one child, maintenance may rise to around 50 to 60 percent of the husband's income.

When there are two or more children, this figure can increase further, sometimes reaching 60 to 70 percent of the monthly income.

This increase ensures the child or children's needs—nutrition, education, healthcare, and general upbringing—are adequately met. The law treats children's welfare as paramount, so maintenance is calculated to sustain their current lifestyle without causing financial strain on the custodial parent.

Case Study: Take the example of Mr. Arjun, a businessman earning ₹1,50,000 monthly. His wife and two children filed for maintenance after separation. Although Arjun argued that his business was running at a loss, the court considered the family's lifestyle – a luxury car, frequent foreign trips, and expensive schooling for the children. The court fixed maintenance at 65% of his income (₹97,500), emphasizing the children's right to maintain their standard of living.

This case highlights a crucial point: even if your declared income seems modest, the court will look at lifestyle indicators and may estimate a higher "imputed" income to calculate maintenance.

Impact of the Wife's Income

If the wife earns a steady income, this can significantly affect maintenance calculations. Courts are increasingly reluctant to grant full maintenance to wives who are financially self-sufficient.

When the wife is employed and earning a reasonable income, the court may reduce maintenance or deny it altogether, especially if she has no children to care for.

However, if she has children, maintenance will usually still be ordered to cover the children's needs, but potentially at a lower amount than if she were unemployed.

The principle here is that maintenance is meant to support dependents who cannot fully support themselves. If the wife is capable of financial independence, the court expects her to contribute towards her own upkeep.

The Supreme Court's Guideline on Arrears

A key judicial development shaping maintenance law is the Supreme Court's ruling in the landmark case Rajnesh vs Neha. The court held that maintenance is payable from the date of filing the petition, not from the date the court passes the order.

This means the husband may accumulate a substantial arrear liability by the time a maintenance order is finalized. These arrears can amount to a large sum, sometimes running into lakhs of rupees, which must be paid in addition to ongoing maintenance. Failure to pay these arrears can lead to severe consequences, including attachment of salary or properties and even imprisonment.

This ruling highlights the importance of early intervention and careful negotiation of interim maintenance, since arrears become enforceable and can create financial burdens that are difficult to overcome later.

Financial and Emotional Costs of Fighting Maintenance

Maintenance proceedings are not only financially demanding but also emotionally taxing. The costs involved in legal fees, repeated court appearances, and the prolonged nature of these cases can take a heavy toll on husbands.

Many men face the difficult decision of whether to settle maintenance claims for a lump sum to avoid escalating legal costs and mental stress, or to engage in full-fledged litigation that could potentially reduce the liability but may drag on for years.

Understanding the cost-benefit analysis of these options is vital. Sometimes, an early settlement—though seemingly costly—may save considerable resources and emotional anguish in the long run.

Real-Life Example

Consider the case of Mr. Sharma (name changed for privacy), a middle-income professional whose wife filed for maintenance shortly after leaving the marital home. The court initially ordered him to pay 40 percent of his in-hand salary as interim maintenance.

Over the next two years, these payments, combined with accrued arrears, became a substantial financial burden. Mr. Sharma sought legal advice and revealed that his wife had a part-time job which was not disclosed in the court filings.

By carefully presenting this evidence and negotiating with the wife's counsel, Mr. Sharma successfully reduced his maintenance liability by nearly 30 percent. This adjustment eased his financial strain and allowed him to regain some stability.

Summary

- Maintenance typically ranges from 30 to 70 percent of the husband's income, depending largely on the wife's employment status and the number of children.
- The presence of children significantly increases maintenance amounts due to their prioritized welfare.
- The wife's earning capacity is a key factor; if she earns, maintenance may be reduced or denied.
- The Supreme Court's ruling in Rajnesh vs Neha makes it mandatory for maintenance payments to begin from the date of petition

filing, resulting in arrears that can be financially challenging.

- Maintenance litigation is expensive and emotionally draining, prompting many husbands to consider settlement versus prolonged fighting.
- Strategic presentation of facts, including uncovering undisclosed income, can help reduce maintenance obligations.

Chapter 3

Inside The Courtroom: Step-By-Step Breakdown of Maintenance Cases

Understanding the procedure in maintenance cases is essential for anyone facing these proceedings. The process can seem complicated and intimidating, but knowing what to expect and when can significantly reduce anxiety and help you prepare effectively.

Whether your case is filed under Section 125 of the Criminal Procedure Code (CrPC) or under the Domestic Violence Act (DV Act), the procedural steps remain largely similar. The maintenance claim begins with a petition or complaint filed by the wife or dependent family member seeking financial support.

Before delving it in the Maintennce factor, let's understand the difference between maintenance in two different laws

Aspect	Maintenance under Domestic Violence (DV) Act	Maintenance under Section 125 CrPC
Purpose	To provide financial relief and protection to victims of domestic violence, including maintenance.	To prevent destitution by providing maintenance to wives, children, and parents who cannot support themselves.
Scope of Beneficiaries	Wife, children, dependent relatives, and any aggrieved person living in a domestic relationship.	Wife, legitimate/unmarried children, and parents unable to maintain themselves.
Type of Relief	Includes maintenance, protection orders, residence orders, and other reliefs related to domestic violence.	Primarily maintenance allowance to the wife, children, or parents.
Procedure	Filed as a complaint under the DV Act; may involve protection officers and Domestic Incident Report (DIR).	Filed as a petition under Section 125 CrPC; straightforward maintenance claim.
Interim Orders	Can grant immediate interim maintenance and protection/residence orders, often ex-parte.	Can grant interim maintenance but no protection or residence orders.
Involvement of Protection Officers	Yes, protection officers investigate and assist in preparing DIRs and ensuring relief.	No role of protection officers; purely judicial process.
Jurisdiction	Can include in-laws and other relatives	Only husband is liable; no in-laws or others.

Aspect	Maintenance under Domestic Violence (DV) Act	Maintenance under Section 125 CrPC
	living in the household.	
Focus	Broader protection against abuse along with financial support.	Solely focused on maintenance and preventing neglect.

FILING THE PETITION

Section 125 of the Criminal Procedure Code (CrPC)

What is Section 125 CrPC?

Section 125 CrPC is a legal provision that allows wives, children, and parents who are unable to maintain themselves to claim monthly maintenance. This section empowers magistrates to order a husband or father to provide financial support, preventing the claimant from falling into destitution.

Purpose

The primary purpose of Section 125 is to provide a quick and effective remedy to financially dependent family members, ensuring they receive basic maintenance without undergoing lengthy litigation. It serves as a safeguard against neglect and abandonment.

Procedure

The claimant files a maintenance petition before the magistrate's court. This petition outlines the claimant's financial needs and the grounds for maintenance. Upon receipt, the court issues a notice to the respondent (usually the husband), requiring him to appear and respond to the claim.

Section 12 of the Protection of Women from Domestic Violence Act, 2005

What is Section 12 DV Act?

Section 12 allows a woman who is a victim of domestic violence to file a complaint seeking protection, maintenance, and other reliefs. Unlike Section 125 CrPC, this Act provides a broader framework addressing physical, emotional, verbal, and economic abuse within a domestic relationship.

Purpose:

The DV Act aims to protect women from all forms of domestic abuse while ensuring their right to live with dignity, which includes receiving adequate financial support. Maintenance under this Act complements other protection measures like residence and protection orders.

Procedure:

A complaint is filed under Section 12 before the magistrate. The court may direct the preparation of a **Domestic Incident Report (DIR)** by a protection officer.

The DIR records the complainant's allegations, including details of abuse and requests for relief.

Role of the Domestic Incident Report (DIR)

The DIR serves as a summary report prepared by the protection officer based on the woman's complaint. Although previously considered mandatory in many courts, recent Supreme Court judgments clarify that a DIR is not essential but may be requested at the court's discretion. It assists the court in assessing the need for interim protection or maintenance orders.

Many husbands, when first served with a complaint under the Domestic Violence Act, believe that the accompanying Domestic Incident Report, or DIR, is the result of a thorough investigation. They imagine that the protection officer has evaluated both sides, assessed the facts, and submitted an unbiased summary to the court. Unfortunately, this assumption is far from the truth.

In reality, the DIR is rarely an investigative report. It is, more often than not, a reproduction of the complainant's allegations. The wife gives her version of events to the protection officer, and the officer, without verifying the facts or hearing the husband's side, transcribes her statements into a standard format. This becomes the DIR—a document that now appears before the court as though it has some official weight. The truth is that it reflects only one side of the story. There is no cross-verification, no evidence analysis, and certainly no opportunity for the husband to be heard at this stage.

To make matters more difficult, the husband is not even entitled to receive a copy of the DIR at this point. It is treated as a document meant solely for the court's consideration. As a result, the husband enters the proceedings already at a disadvantage, unaware of what has been written about him, and unable to respond until he is served with a notice.

Once the complaint is filed—whether under the Domestic Violence Act or Section 125 of the Criminal Procedure Code—the court issues notice to the respondent. In cases filed under the Domestic Violence Act, it is common for notices to be sent not just to the husband, but also to his parents or relatives if they have been named in the complaint. However, under Section 125 Cr.P.C., only the husband is made a party, and only he is called upon to respond.

At this early stage, one of the first things the husband should check is whether the complaint has been filed in the appropriate jurisdiction. It is not uncommon for wives to file complaints in courts where they are not ordinary residents, simply to cause inconvenience or to gain a perceived legal advantage. If the case has been filed in an improper forum, the husband can raise an objection on the ground of territorial jurisdiction. This must be done before submitting a formal reply. In some cases, this objection alone can lead to dismissal or transfer of the case.

What many are unaware of is the concept of ad interim maintenance, which, though not specifically mentioned in the law, is regularly applied in practice. In cases where the wife is not working and has a child, courts often award temporary maintenance on the very first date of hearing. This may range anywhere from ten to twenty thousand rupees per month, depending on the husband's income. The amount can be fixed even before the husband has a chance to file his reply. This early order is intended to provide immediate financial relief, but in doing so, it imposes an obligation before any proper hearing has taken place.

In addition to ad interim maintenance, domestic violence cases carry another challenge: ex parte orders. Even before the husband appears in court, the wife can obtain orders for residence, protection, or maintenance under Section 23 of the Domestic Violence Act. These ex parte orders are granted based solely on her statements, and they remain in effect until a final decision is made or the husband successfully contests them. Once the wife's interim application under Section 23 is heard and decided, that order takes precedence over any earlier ad interim orders. These early decisions—passed in the absence of any reply or evidence from the husband—can have serious consequences.

Eventually, the husband gets the opportunity to file his reply. This is a critical point in the case. In the reply, he must lay out his full defense, present any documents, and respond to each of the allegations raised in the complaint. This reply often sets the tone for how the rest of the proceedings will unfold.

After the reply is filed, the court typically directs both parties to submit detailed income affidavits. This practice stems from the Supreme Court's guidelines in the Rajnesh vs Neha judgment. These affidavits must disclose all relevant financial details—monthly income, savings, investments, loans, liabilities, and even bank statements—for the past three years. The purpose is to help the court fairly assess the financial condition of both parties before determining the maintenance amount.

This is where the next layer of complication arises. It is common for one or both parties to hide income or exaggerate expenses. A wife may claim to be unemployed while working under the table or earning in cash. A husband may underreport his earnings or inflate his liabilities. In either case, such concealment distorts the court's assessment and often leads to unfair maintenance orders. It becomes essential at this stage to expose any false claims, using appropriate legal tools to bring the truth to light.

The early phase of a maintenance case is where most of the damage—or defense—is done. Orders passed in the beginning, often without the husband's side being fully heard, can create long-term consequences that are difficult to reverse. Understanding this process and responding strategically is key to navigating maintenance litigation effectively and avoiding avoidable setbacks.

Now, let us delve into one of the most strategic tools available to a husband during maintenance proceedings: the application under Section 91 of the Criminal Procedure Code. This provision becomes especially powerful when there is a reasonable suspicion that the wife is concealing critical financial information, such as income from employment or hidden assets.

Section 91 allows the court to summon documents or records from third parties if those documents are necessary for the case. To effectively use this provision, the husband does not need to possess complete documentation. Basic details are sufficient. For instance, if the husband has reason to believe that the wife is employed at a certain company or is maintaining a bank account at a particular branch, that information alone can be used to initiate a Section 91 application. It is important to clarify here that there is no need to obtain documents through illegal means. The purpose is not to conduct private surveillance, but to use the legal process to obtain truthful evidence through the court.

In one of my cases, the wife categorically denied being employed. However, we had information about her previous workplace. Based on that, we filed a Section 91 application, merely stating the employer's name. The court, acting on its own motion, summoned her employment details, including salary slips and appointment records. Once confronted with these documents, the wife had no option but to admit her employment, and as a result, the court dismissed her maintenance application.

In another case, we discovered that the wife was working in Gurugram and had a known salary account at a particular bank. With only these basic inputs, we requested the court to summon the relevant bank and salary documents under Section 91. The information confirmed regular income. Since the wife had concealed this fact in her affidavit, her maintenance claim was dismissed, and the court ordered zero maintenance.

These examples highlight how powerful Section 91 can be when used strategically. If the documents obtained contradict the sworn statements made by the wife, it not only damages her credibility but also opens the door for perjury proceedings. According to Section 340 of the CrPC, if a person makes false statements on oath or conceals material facts, they can be prosecuted for perjury. Once incriminating documents are on record that establish that the wife misled the court under oath, it is the appropriate time to file a Section 340 application.

Recent judgments have clarified that when a Section 340 application is filed, it must be considered and decided before the main case proceeds further. This ensures that the falsehood is addressed before it leads to an unjust outcome. Filing a Section 340 application at this stage not only puts pressure on the complainant to come clean but also strengthens the husband's position significantly in the eyes of the court.

Once the income affidavits are on record, and if the husband has successfully challenged any concealment, the case moves to the stage of deciding interim maintenance. Interim maintenance applications are filed under Section 125 of the CrPC or Section 23 of the Domestic Violence Act. At this juncture, the court hears arguments from both parties regarding the amount of financial support that may be awarded temporarily until the final decision.

If it is proven or reasonably suspected that the wife is employed and has willfully suppressed this information, it gives a strategic advantage to the husband. Courts have repeatedly held that a woman who is qualified and capable of earning should make efforts to support herself. If she voluntarily chooses not to work, she cannot expect to become a lifelong financial burden on the husband.

Where the wife is earning and has no children, the court may either deny maintenance altogether or grant a nominal amount. However, when a minor child is involved, the court typically leans towards ensuring adequate support for the child. Even if the wife is earning, the husband may still be directed to provide maintenance to cover the child's expenses, such as school fees, medical care, and daily needs.

Another important factor that courts consider while deciding maintenance is the actual in-hand salary of the husband. Merely showing high expenses or personal loans will not help reduce the maintenance amount. The court expects clarity and proof. Deductions such as income tax and statutory contributions may be taken into account, as well as responsibilities like supporting aged or ailing parents. However, the court does not view favorably any attempt to avoid financial liability by claiming self-induced unemployment. Quitting a job voluntarily, or deliberately reducing income, will not be considered valid grounds for reducing maintenance.

Once the interim maintenance order is passed, the case progresses to the evidence stage. At this point, the wife submits her evidence in the form of an affidavit, attaching supporting documents such as bills, certificates, salary slips (if claiming unemployment), and photographs. This affidavit is marked and exhibited during proceedings. The husband then gets the opportunity to cross-examine her. This stage is crucial, as the cross-examination allows the husband to question inconsistencies, expose falsehoods, and test the credibility of the wife's claims.

Following this, the husband may also submit his own evidence in the form of an affidavit, along with documents supporting his defense—such as proof of expenses, dependents, medical records of parents, or any documents disproving the wife's claims. Once both sides have submitted and marked their evidence, the matter is listed for final arguments.

During final arguments, both parties summarize their positions and address the court on the merits of the case. The judge then deliberates on the evidence, income affidavits, legal submissions, and other factors before passing the final maintenance order. From start to finish, this entire process—from the first hearing to the final decision—often takes a minimum of three to four years, depending on the court's workload and the complexity of the case.

Therefore, navigating maintenance proceedings requires not only legal knowledge but strategic planning, timely action, and a clear understanding of procedural tools. The effective use of provisions like Section 91 and Section 340 CrPC can change the course of a case and prevent unjust financial burdens that arise from false or exaggerated claims

Chapter 4

What The Judge Sees: How Maintenance Amounts Are Decided

Maintenance proceedings, whether interim or final, are crucial facets of matrimonial litigation. The primary aim is to ensure that a spouse, who is unable to maintain themselves, is provided with adequate financial support by the other. Courts across India rely on a variety of parameters to determine the quantum of maintenance to be awarded. This chapter delves into those parameters with a particular focus on the assessment of income, standard of living, and the evidentiary burden placed on both parties, especially the husband.

The first and foremost factor that courts consider while determining maintenance is the income of the husband. This evaluation, however, is not as straightforward as it appears. While salaried individuals may find it relatively easier to present evidence of income, individuals engaged in businesses or professions often present complexities, especially when they underreport earnings or declare business losses. Consequently, courts have developed jurisprudence that goes beyond mere paperwork to assess the true financial capability of a party.

Income of the Husband: The Starting Point

In most maintenance claims, the inquiry begins with assessing the monthly income of the husband. Courts often direct the husband to furnish a detailed income affidavit, supported by documentary proof. For salaried individuals, this typically includes six months' salary slips, three years' bank statements, and a copy of the income tax returns. These documents help the court ascertain the regular monthly inflow of income and identify any discrepancies between reported income and actual lifestyle.

However, it is essential to recognize that these documents do not always paint the full picture. In some cases, husbands may attempt to manipulate the figures by showing inflated deductions, concealing perks or allowances, or transferring income-generating assets to family members. The courts, in such cases, adopt a practical approach by considering not just the documentary evidence, but also circumstantial indicators that reflect the real financial standing.

The situation becomes more complex when the husband is self-employed, runs a business, or is involved in a family enterprise. In such cases, income is often not regular, and business losses may be shown deliberately to escape the obligation of paying maintenance. Courts are well aware of such tactics and have repeatedly held that income tax returns and profit and loss statements, although relevant, are not conclusive proof of actual income.

For instance, a husband running a family business may declare a nominal salary or dividend as his income, while in reality, he may be enjoying a lavish lifestyle funded by the business. In many judgments, courts have emphasized that the lifestyle of the parties, their spending habits, and their assets must be considered to arrive at a fair estimation of income. The burden thus shifts on the husband to disprove any allegations made by the wife regarding his actual financial capacity.

Let us understand this with a practical example. In one case, a husband declared his monthly income as a mere ₹6,000, presenting job slips as evidence. However, it was brought to the court's notice that he was associated with a flourishing family business and was actively working alongside his father. The wife provided photographic and documentary evidence of the husband driving a high-end luxury vehicle, using premium mobile phones, and living in an upscale locality. Furthermore, she presented investment documents showing substantial amounts in the husband's name. The court found it implausible that a person with such a lifestyle could subsist on ₹6,000 per month. It accordingly invoked the doctrine of 'constructive income' and estimated the husband's real income using judicial guesswork, ultimately fixing the maintenance at ₹1,00,000 per month. This decision was based on the principle that the husband's financial lifestyle contradicted the income he claimed to earn.

The Relevance of Lifestyle and Expenditure

In assessing the quantum of maintenance, the court not only looks at the actual income but also the standard of living enjoyed by both spouses during the subsistence of the marriage. This is grounded in the principle that the wife is entitled to maintain the same standard of living she enjoyed while residing with the husband.

There are cases where husbands report heavy business losses but continue to incur large expenditures on luxury items or international travel. In such scenarios, the court reasonably presumes that if a person can afford such expenditures, they are capable of paying maintenance. In one such matter, a husband declared losses of ₹10,00,000 per month from his business venture. Despite these losses, he continued to maintain luxury vehicles, held multiple credit cards with high spending limits, and paid substantial school fees for his children from a previous relationship. The court observed that a person suffering massive losses would not be able to sustain such a lifestyle unless he had undisclosed sources of income. Consequently, the court fixed a monthly maintenance amount of ₹1,00,000, observing that someone who can afford to lose such huge sums in business can certainly afford to maintain his spouse.

This approach underscores a critical aspect of maintenance litigation—the courts are not bound by the income shown in books of account alone. They have the discretion to draw reasonable inferences from the standard of living, properties owned, loans availed, credit card statements, utility bills, and similar indicators. Thus, husbands seeking to underplay their income may unwittingly reveal their financial standing through their lifestyle and consumption patterns.

Assessing Maintenance in NRI and Foreign Income Cases

Another significant dimension is the case of Non-Resident Indians (NRIs) or persons living abroad. Maintenance proceedings involving NRIs often raise intricate issues concerning parity in the standard of living. While a person earning in dollars, pounds, or euros may claim that the wife, living in a rural part of India, does not require maintenance based on foreign cost-of-living standards, courts have routinely held otherwise.

The rationale adopted is that if the husband enjoys a high standard of living abroad, the wife should not be made to suffer merely because she resides in a less expensive area. The court attempts to strike a balance—while not awarding maintenance in absolute dollar terms, it considers the overall parity of lifestyle. For example, a husband residing in the United Kingdom and earning £5,000 per month may claim that the wife requires only ₹15,000 to ₹20,000 if she resides in rural India. However, courts have observed that the wife is entitled to a standard of living proportionate to that of the husband, and hence, maintenance may be fixed at ₹1,00,000 or more, depending on the circumstances. While the exact quantum is adjusted according to the region and cost-of-living disparity, the guiding principle remains that of maintaining lifestyle parity.

Evasion by Concealment or Underreporting by Either Spouse

Just as husbands may underreport income, there have been numerous instances where the wife, despite being qualified and employable, does not disclose her income or employment potential. Courts have recognized this trend and have started evaluating the wife's educational background, work experience, and the prevailing job market to arrive at a notional income.

In such cases, if the wife is found to be well-qualified—say, a postgraduate or professionally trained individual—who chooses to remain unemployed without sufficient justification, courts have presumed a notional income based on industry standards. The principle applied is that a capable person cannot voluntarily sit idle and claim maintenance when they are otherwise employable. However, the actual presumption depends on whether the wife was working during the marriage, whether she had to leave the job due to domestic responsibilities, and her current efforts to find employment.

On the other hand, if the husband is unemployed or claims to have no income, the court does not allow this as a ground for avoiding maintenance. Instead, it assumes that at the very least, the husband is capable of earning the minimum wages applicable in the jurisdiction. This assumption provides a baseline for awarding maintenance and ensures that the obligation is not defeated by evasive conduct.

Status of the Parties and Maintenance Calculation

While income is a vital factor, the overall status of the parties—defined by their educational background, family wealth, lifestyle, and past expenditure habits—also plays a critical role. For instance, in families where the marriage occurred in a well-to-do setup with expensive gifts, international travel, or luxurious weddings, courts presume that the parties belong to a certain social strata. In such situations, even if the husband's income temporarily drops or is difficult to prove, the court may still order a substantial maintenance to maintain the parity in lifestyle.

Similarly, the presence of ancestral properties, agricultural income, family business revenues, and shareholdings in companies also inform the court's decision. Although such income may not be directly credited to the husband's bank account, the court can infer financial strength based on these holdings.

Judicial Discretion and Estimation (Guesswork)

Ultimately, the court has wide discretion in fixing maintenance. While this discretion is exercised judiciously, it often involves educated estimation or guesswork in the absence of direct proof. This power is not arbitrary—it is derived from the court's responsibility to ensure justice and avoid hardship to either party. Courts frequently rely on judicial precedents, lifestyle assessments, income approximations, and parity principles to make such estimations.

In conclusion, maintenance is not fixed on a rigid formula. While documentary evidence is crucial, it is the totality of circumstances—including lifestyle, expenditure, concealment tactics, and standard of living—that determines the final amount. Husbands defending against maintenance claims must therefore be cautious in presenting an honest and consistent picture of their finances. Concealing assets or underreporting income can result in adverse inferences, leading to higher maintenance awards.

For husbands facing such claims, the strategy must involve not only producing authentic financial documents but also contesting exaggerated claims of the wife, highlighting her qualifications, employability, and any income she may be receiving. The objective is not merely to reduce liability but to ensure that the maintenance awarded is fair, just, and proportionate to the real needs and capacities of both parties.

Another common scenario encountered in maintenance proceedings is where the husband pleads unemployment or job loss as a reason for being unable to pay maintenance. While this may appear to be a valid defense at first glance, Indian courts have consistently held that mere unemployment is not an adequate ground to evade the legal obligation to support one's spouse or child. In such cases, the judiciary has evolved a practical approach by considering the husband's last drawn salary as a benchmark for assessing his earning capacity.

The rationale behind this approach is rooted in the presumption that the husband, if he had continued in a normal marital relationship, would have utilized his past income or existing savings to maintain the standard of living of the family. Therefore, the court does not accept a blanket assertion of zero income as a defense. Instead, the financial parameters are evaluated on the basis of the last known income and the standard of living previously enjoyed by the parties.

In one illustrative case, the husband had been earning ₹1,00,000 per month prior to his alleged unemployment. During the proceedings, he submitted that he had lost his job and was therefore incapable of providing any maintenance. However, the court did not accept this argument. It noted that loss of employment, without any credible effort to secure alternative income, does not absolve a person of his responsibility. Furthermore, it observed that individuals are expected to manage their obligations even during temporary periods of financial distress, especially when they are otherwise educated, employable, and capable of earning.

What made this case more interesting was that the wife was also employed and was earning nearly half of what the husband was previously drawing. Despite this, the court awarded maintenance in favor of the wife and the minor child. The judgment emphasized that comparative earnings and responsibilities must be examined holistically. Even though the wife had some income, it did not negate the husband's duty, particularly when the standard of living during the marriage was largely maintained through his earnings. The court also took into account the child's needs and the economic disparity between the parties.

This example underlines an important judicial principle: the obligation to pay maintenance does not vanish simply because the husband is currently out of employment. The court may presume that he has access to other sources—be it savings, severance packages, family support, or even temporary earnings—and therefore remains financially capable to fulfill his legal duties. Moreover, if the husband is qualified and experienced, courts expect him to take proactive steps to secure alternative employment. Failure to do so may even be seen as a deliberate attempt to avoid financial responsibility.

Therefore, in cases where the husband pleads job loss, the legal strategy must be carefully devised. The husband must not only prove his unemployment but also show credible, consistent efforts to regain employment. If the husband is in a field where alternative work is readily available or if he possesses significant experience or qualifications, the court may disregard the unemployment plea altogether. The principle is that one cannot willfully remain unemployed or underemployed to escape maintenance liabilities.

At the same time, if the wife is earning, her income will be considered to assess the need and quantum of maintenance. However, as the aforementioned case illustrates, the wife's earning capacity does not automatically disentitle her from receiving support. The concept of comparative financial strength, standard of living, and responsibilities such as child care continue to be crucial considerations.

In conclusion, pleading unemployment is not a foolproof defense in maintenance proceedings. Courts focus on earning potential, past income, and lifestyle rather than taking the claim of job loss at face value. Husbands who raise this plea must be prepared to demonstrate their genuine financial incapacity and sustained efforts toward regaining employment. Otherwise, the last drawn salary and overall capacity will be presumed, and maintenance will be awarded accordingly

Chapter 5

Unmasking The Hidden Income: The Art of Evidence Discovery

In maintenance proceedings under matrimonial law, one of the critical issues that frequently arises is the concealment or misrepresentation of income, assets, and financial capacity by either party. Whether it is the husband or the wife, parties often attempt to understate their earnings or hide valuable assets to manipulate the outcome of the maintenance order. This tendency, although not uncommon, can lead to serious legal consequences and is considered a misuse of the judicial process. The courts have taken note of this behavior and have evolved certain legal mechanisms to curb such practices, ensuring fairness and transparency in determining maintenance.

A landmark case in this context is the Supreme Court judgment in *Rajnish v. Neha* (2021), which provided comprehensive guidelines on the disclosure of income and assets in maintenance cases. In this judgment, the Hon'ble Supreme Court emphasized the necessity of filing a detailed income affidavit by both parties to ensure a fair assessment of financial capacity. The Court introduced a structured format for the income affidavit to be filed by both the husband and the wife, covering all relevant aspects such as salary, business income, real estate, movable and immovable properties, bank account details, investments, liabilities, and standard of living.

The rationale behind such detailed disclosure is simple: maintenance is awarded based on a realistic appraisal of the financial condition of both parties. If one party, typically the husband in most cases, hides substantial income or assets, the maintenance amount may be unfairly reduced. On the other hand, if the wife conceals her own income or earning capacity, it may result in unjust enrichment and undue financial burden on the husband. Therefore, complete and truthful disclosure is indispensable for justice.

Unfortunately, in many real-life cases, parties do not comply fully with these guidelines. For instance, spouses often operate multiple bank accounts, of which only a select few are disclosed. High-value transactions in hidden accounts, significant investments in mutual funds, shares, fixed deposits, or ownership of properties held in the name of relatives or shell entities are commonly concealed. Additionally, in cases where the spouse is employed in the private sector or self-employed in business, they may declare a lower salary or loss-making financial position despite enjoying a high standard of living.

To counter this, the law provides remedies. One such powerful provision is Section 91 of the Code of Criminal Procedure, 1973 (CrPC), which can be invoked by either party during maintenance proceedings. Under Section 91 CrPC, a party may file an application before the court seeking the production of specific documents or records relevant to the case. These documents may include salary slips, bank statements, income tax returns, property records, employment details, and investment proofs.

Certainly. Section 91 of the Code of Criminal Procedure, 1973, provides a mechanism for a court or an officer in charge of a police station to summon any person to produce documents or other items that are considered necessary or desirable for the purposes of an investigation, inquiry, trial, or any other proceeding. This provision empowers the court to order the production of relevant evidence or records that may be crucial in determining the facts of the case. The person who receives such a summons is legally obligated to comply unless there is a valid legal reason to refuse, such as privilege or confidentiality. This section is often invoked when one party believes that the other is concealing important documents or evidence that could influence the outcome of the case.

In the context of maintenance proceedings, Section 91 is a powerful tool to obtain financial documents like bank statements, salary slips, income tax returns, property ownership papers, or records related to investments and business transactions. If one spouse suspects that the other has hidden assets or underreported income, they can request the court to issue a summons under this section to compel the production of such documents. The court, upon being satisfied about the relevance of these documents, can direct the concerned person or institution, such as a bank or employer, to produce them. This helps the court arrive at a fair and just decision by revealing the true financial position of the parties involved. Non-compliance with such an order can lead to legal consequences and adverse inferences by the court. Thus, Section 91 serves as an important procedural provision to ensure transparency and truthfulness in legal proceedings.

The process under Section 91 CrPC is initiated after the parties file their income affidavits. If one party suspects that the other has withheld or suppressed crucial information, they may file a formal application under this section. The applicant must specify the nature of the documents sought and the relevance of such information. For example, if a wife claims that the husband owns undisclosed properties or holds multiple bank accounts, she may file a 91 CrPC application requesting the court to summon documents from the relevant banks or property registration authorities.

The court, upon being satisfied with the prima facie merit of the application, may issue directions to the concerned authority or employer to produce the relevant records. These records can significantly alter the course of the proceedings by revealing the true financial status of the party. For example, bank statements may show unexplained deposits, luxurious expenditure, or recurring credits, indicating a higher income than what was claimed. Similarly, income tax returns or Form 26AS can reveal additional income sources such as rent, dividends, or business income.

In addition to Section 91 CrPC, the court also has the power to draw adverse inferences against a party who deliberately withholds information or fails to comply with the direction of the court. Non-disclosure can be interpreted as a sign of dishonesty and may lead the court to assume the income and asset value based on circumstantial evidence, lifestyle indicators, and other materials placed on record. For instance, the court may take into account photographs of a lavish wedding, possession of luxury vehicles, foreign travel records, or high-end mobile phones as indicators of substantial financial means.

However, the repercussions do not stop there. If it is found that a party has deliberately lied under oath or has submitted false documents, the aggrieved party can move a separate application under Section 340 of the CrPC. This provision deals with perjury—the act of making false statements in judicial proceedings. The filing of a false income affidavit, suppression of material facts, or submission of forged documents can attract proceedings under this section.

Section 340 CrPC empowers the court to initiate criminal proceedings against the erring party for committing offences punishable under sections of the Indian Penal Code, such as Section 193 (false evidence), Section 199 (false statement made in declaration), and

Section 209 (fraudulently bringing false claims before a court). Once such an application is filed and found to be maintainable, the court may conduct a preliminary inquiry and, if satisfied, may lodge a complaint with the magistrate having jurisdiction to try such offences. The consequence may include imprisonment and fine, and more importantly, a permanent dent on the credibility of the party.

It is crucial to understand that the courts do not take such acts lightly. The judicial system relies on the integrity of affidavits and the truthfulness of parties. Misleading the court is considered an abuse of the process of law and is viewed with utmost seriousness. Even if perjury proceedings are not initiated, the court may penalize the party by denying relief or by enhancing the maintenance amount using guesswork, thereby defeating the very purpose of concealment.

It is also worth noting that third-party disclosures may become relevant in these proceedings. For example, if a husband claims to be unemployed but is receiving regular credits in his bank account from a company, the wife may move a Section 91 CrPC application to call for records from the company showing salary payments or professional fees. Likewise, if the wife claims no income but is engaged in consultancy, freelancing, or owns a boutique, her bank statements or client communications can be summoned to assess the actual income.

Another important aspect is the role of digital and electronic evidence. In today's era, evidence such as WhatsApp messages, emails, social media posts, and online transaction records can also provide crucial insights into the lifestyle and financial transactions of the parties. For instance, frequent shopping on luxury portals, international trips posted on social media, or communication with clients regarding payments may become relevant in determining the income and expenditure.

In maintenance proceedings involving Non-Resident Indians (NRIs), this issue becomes even more complex. NRIs often do not disclose their foreign assets or income. However, courts have been increasingly proactive in such matters. If the spouse is earning in a foreign currency and living in a developed nation, the court may consider the standard of living there and expect proportionate maintenance for the wife and children, even if the wife resides in India. In such cases, foreign tax returns, bank statements, and employment records can be sought either through mutual legal assistance treaties (MLATs) or by initiating Section 91 CrPC applications, subject to the court's satisfaction.

The guiding principle in all such cases remains transparency, fairness, and a realistic approach to financial status. Both parties are expected to come with clean hands. It is advisable not to withhold material facts or mislead the court. Lawyers must advise their clients accordingly, as concealing information is a double-edged sword. In the short term, it may delay or reduce the maintenance, but in the long term, it can backfire disastrously with adverse orders, penalties, and criminal prosecution.

To conclude, the legal framework offers robust tools such as detailed income affidavits, Section 91 CrPC applications, and Section 340 CrPC proceedings to uncover the truth behind financial disclosures. Parties involved in maintenance disputes should be well aware of the consequences of misrepresentation. Full disclosure is not just a legal obligation but also a strategic necessity to avoid adverse judicial outcomes. Maintenance law, while aiming to protect the vulnerable spouse, also imposes duties of honesty and cooperation on both sides. Any deviation from these principles is bound to be met with strict legal repercussions.

Chapter 6

What Really Counts: Expenses That Can Make or Break Your Case

Expenses considered by courts when deciding maintenance cases are a crucial factor in determining the husband's financial capacity to support his wife and children. It is important to understand that courts do not simply accept any claim of financial inability by the husband, especially when such claims involve monthly obligations like EMIs for cars or houses. Husbands often argue that they lack sufficient liquidity due to these expenses, or that their financial responsibilities towards elderly and ailing parents restrict their ability to pay maintenance. However, the courts take a pragmatic approach, scrutinizing all such expenses closely before arriving at a decision.

For instance, in one notable case, a husband was ordered by the court to pay a maintenance amount of Rs. 40,000 per month to his elderly parents. Later, he argued that this obligation made it impossible for him to pay maintenance to his wife and child. The court rejected this argument outright, reasoning that if he could afford to pay Rs. 40,000 monthly to his parents, he certainly had the means to contribute to the maintenance of his wife and child. This judgment highlights the court's position that obligations towards parents do not override or negate the primary duty towards the wife and children. This principle reflects a well-established hierarchy in maintenance obligations under Indian law, where the husband's responsibility towards his wife and children takes precedence.

When assessing expenses, courts differentiate between essential and discretionary spending. Essential expenses include things like legitimate EMIs on housing and vehicles, statutory deductions such as provident fund contributions and taxes, medical expenses for dependents, and necessary business expenses. Discretionary spending—such as lavish personal expenditures, expensive vacations, and luxury purchases—is generally scrutinized and often disregarded when evaluating the husband's ability to pay maintenance. If a husband claims he cannot pay maintenance due to high EMIs but is found spending lavishly on himself, courts are likely to discredit such claims. Similarly, in business cases where the husband reports heavy losses but continues to pay large salaries or maintain a high lifestyle, courts will consider these factors negatively against him.

Business owners often try to show low or no income by inflating business expenses or declaring losses. Courts, however, are aware of such tactics and rely on indirect evidence to determine the husband's actual financial capacity. This includes examining lifestyle indicators such as ownership of luxury vehicles, multiple properties, frequent travel, and investments. Courts may also review payment records to employees or contractors and conduct bank account analyses. This comprehensive approach helps prevent false declarations and ensures maintenance amounts are fixed fairly in line with the husband's real means.

In maintenance proceedings, courts usually assess the husband's net income rather than gross income. Net income is calculated after deducting statutory obligations such as Employees' Provident Fund (EPF) contributions, income tax, and professional tax. Courts may also consider other necessary deductions like medical insurance premiums, provided they are non-voluntary and essential. However, voluntary or discretionary expenses are not accepted as valid deductions against maintenance liability.

To give a clearer perspective, here is a table summarizing the average deductions courts typically accept against gross income in maintenance cases:

Type of Expense	Average Deduction Percentage of Gross Income	Notes
Housing Loan EMI	15%	Not considered
Vehicle Loan EMI	5%	Not considered

Type of Expense	Average Deduction Percentage of Gross Income	Notes
Statutory Deductions	20%	Includes EPF, income tax, professional tax considered
Medical Expenses	3%	Includes insurance premiums and necessary treatment partly considered
Parental Maintenance	Variable (5-15%)	Based on legal orders or actual need and considered
Discretionary Spending	Typically not accepted	Courts scrutinize luxury expenses

This breakdown shows that while statutory deductions and EMIs constitute a substantial part of deductions, courts remain skeptical about discretionary expenses and usually exclude them from consideration.

Courts also carefully evaluate the legitimacy of claimed loan EMIs and rental expenses. If the husband has taken loans for housing or vehicles, and the EMIs are reasonable and consistent with his income, such expenses are accepted as genuine. However, courts inquire if the loan was taken for family benefit and whether the husband prioritizes these payments over maintenance obligations. If the husband owns multiple properties but claims high rental expenses, courts may reject or reduce these claims after verifying rental agreements or payment proofs. Generally EMI supports lifestyle and will negatively impacts husband

Maintenance obligations towards elderly parents also factor into court calculations, but with important limitations. While legal provisions like the Maintenance and Welfare of Parents and Senior Citizens Act, 2007, require a husband to maintain his parents, this duty does not absolve him from his primary responsibility to support his wife and children. Courts maintain that even if the husband is paying parental maintenance, he must fulfill his family obligations first. The ability to pay maintenance to parents is considered an indicator of the husband's financial capacity, which should reflect in his ability to pay maintenance to the wife and children as well.

Another significant factor courts consider is the standard of living and lifestyle the husband maintains. The wife and children are entitled to a lifestyle reasonably comparable to what was enjoyed during the marriage. This means if the husband owns luxury cars, lives in an upscale rented house, or travels frequently, the wife and children are entitled to maintenance that enables them to maintain a similar standard of living. Courts often rely on tangible lifestyle evidence such as vehicle ownership, property records, spending on clothing and utilities, and travel history. This lifestyle-based approach helps courts look beyond declared incomes and identify discrepancies that point to concealed income or inflated expenses.

Concealing income or overstating expenses can have serious consequences. Courts have powers under Section 91 of the Criminal Procedure Code to order discovery and production of documents if there is suspicion of hidden assets or undeclared income. Additionally, parties found lying to the court can face proceedings under Section 340 CrPC for perjury, which carries penalties including imprisonment and fines. Courts are empowered to draw adverse inferences against parties who withhold financial information, and maintenance amounts may be fixed based on indirect evidence or guesswork, often resulting in higher awards.

To illustrate the disparity courts often encounter between declared income and actual financial capacity, consider the following table:

Case No.	Declared Monthly Income (₹)	Lifestyle Estimated Monthly Income (₹)	Maintenance Fixed (₹)
1	15,000	1,20,000	90,000
2	50,000	80,000	60,000
3	10,000	1,00,000	75,000
4	1,00,000	1,50,000	1,20,000

This data shows that courts often set maintenance based on lifestyle and estimated financial capacity rather than declared income alone, especially where income concealment is suspected.

In summary, courts carefully balance the husband's declared expenses and income with objective lifestyle indicators and legal obligations. While loan EMIs, statutory deductions, and parental maintenance are accepted to an extent, courts do not allow these to become shields to evade maintenance. Discretionary spending and lifestyle evidence are heavily weighted to ensure maintenance awards are just and reflect the husband's true financial ability. Concealment of income or assets invites stringent judicial action and may backfire on the party attempting to mislead the court. Ultimately, the goal is to secure a fair and dignified maintenance allowance for the wife and children consistent with the husband's means and family standards

Chapter 7

Zero Rupee Game: Strategies To Eliminate or Slash Maintenance

Many individuals, especially those navigating the difficult waters of matrimonial disputes, often approach maintenance cases with a great deal of apprehension and concern. A common scenario that stirs considerable anxiety is when a wife voluntarily leaves the marital home and later files a complaint alleging domestic violence, subsequently seeking maintenance from the husband. This situation, fraught with emotional and legal complexities, frequently leaves husbands worried about the financial obligations courts might impose upon them. However, understanding the legal framework that governs maintenance cases can provide clarity and offer strategic avenues to address such claims effectively.

It is important to note that maintenance laws in India, including provisions under the Hindu Marriage Act, the Protection of Women from Domestic Violence Act, and various other statutes, aim primarily to protect the rights and welfare of the spouse and children who may be financially weaker. Nevertheless, courts are also mindful of the facts and circumstances surrounding each case and ensure that maintenance orders are just, equitable, and aligned with the true financial capacities of the parties involved.

One successful legal strategy that has emerged in certain cases involves meticulous presentation of evidence and a thorough financial audit of both spouses. This approach, although not universally applicable—especially in cases involving children or genuine hardship—can significantly reduce or even nullify maintenance obligations when implemented with precision. The cornerstone of this strategy is a robust compilation and presentation of financial information to demonstrate the actual economic status of both the husband and wife.

The first and arguably most crucial step in this strategy is the provision of comprehensive financial information. This involves gathering detailed documentation such as bank statements spanning several years, income tax returns, salary slips, investment portfolios, loan statements, and records of any significant financial transactions. Merely providing superficial or partial financial records is inadequate; courts expect full transparency and disclosure. The aim is to create an accurate, transparent financial profile that allows the court to understand the genuine financial standing of both parties.

Legal procedures play a vital role in obtaining such documentation formally and ensuring that they are placed on record. Instead of directly seeking documents from financial institutions or employers, parties should utilize statutory provisions like Section 91 of the Criminal Procedure Code (CrPC), which empowers courts to summon persons or compel the production of documents necessary for the case. By filing a Section 91 application, parties can legally and formally request banks, companies, or other entities to disclose relevant financial records. This process not only lends credibility to the case but also shields the party seeking documents from claims of harassment or illegal data gathering.

An essential element of this strategy is emphasizing the financial independence and earning capacity of the wife. Courts have consistently held that maintenance is not automatically guaranteed if the wife is capable of earning an adequate income but chooses not to. If the wife is well-educated, qualified, and physically fit to work but deliberately avoids employment or conceals alternative income sources, her claim for maintenance is significantly weakened. In fact, the courts expect spouses to make reasonable efforts to become self-sufficient and only grant maintenance to the extent that the claimant genuinely cannot support themselves.

Closely tied to this is the careful scrutiny of the wife's declared expenses and liabilities. A common tactic in some maintenance claims is inflating expenses or presenting dubious financial liabilities to create an impression of financial need. Courts are vigilant about such inconsistencies. If the wife fails to provide convincing explanations or proof of how these expenses are being met, her credibility suffers. Discrepancies between her bank transactions and declared liabilities often lead the court to question the veracity of her entire claim.

The court's approach in these matters is holistic. It weighs numerous factors before arriving at a decision, including the financial capabilities of both parties, existing debts or liabilities, the standard of living enjoyed during the marriage, and whether there are dependent children or other family members. When the wife is found capable of earning and deliberately withholds information about income or assets, courts may dismiss or reduce maintenance awards to prevent misuse of the legal system.

In one illustrative case, the wife had left the marital home, alleging domestic violence, and sought maintenance. However, upon detailed examination of her financial transactions, the husband's legal team uncovered significant, unexplained deposits and expenditures. Using a Section 91 application, they compelled the production of bank statements and income documents, which revealed that the wife was not only financially stable but had substantial independent income. Her failure to disclose this information during the proceedings gravely affected her credibility. The court, after considering the comprehensive evidence, ruled in favor of the husband, awarding zero maintenance. The absence of children and any disabilities on her part further supported the court's decision. This case stands as a precedent for how diligent fact-finding and legal acumen can dramatically influence the outcome of maintenance claims.

The success of this strategy hinges on detailed evidence gathering and strict adherence to legal procedures. It sends a clear message that frivolous or exaggerated claims will not be entertained and that the court seeks genuine need and fairness in awarding maintenance. Equally important is the emphasis on transparency—concealing financial information or providing false affidavits invites severe judicial consequences, including contempt of court or perjury charges.

In another noteworthy example, a wife sought interim maintenance from her husband while the main proceedings were ongoing. She claimed unemployment and financial incapacity to support herself. However, the husband, suspecting concealment, filed a Section 91 application to uncover her true employment status. The court ordered the production of her employment records, which revealed she was actively employed and earning a respectable income. This critical discovery not only discredited her affidavit but also exposed her intent to mislead the court. Consequently, the judge dismissed her claim for interim maintenance, underscoring the importance of honesty and full disclosure in maintenance matters.

This case illustrates the court's firm stance against attempts to manipulate financial disclosures. Interim maintenance, meant to provide immediate relief, is nonetheless subject to scrutiny, and false claims can result in loss of credibility and adverse orders. The court's insistence on transparency ensures that all parties meet their legal responsibilities in good faith.

From a broader perspective, these examples highlight the necessity for spouses facing maintenance claims to engage competent legal counsel capable of navigating complex financial investigations and procedural nuances. Successful management of such cases often involves forensic accountants, legal experts in family law, and sometimes even private investigators to establish the true financial status of the parties.

For those on the receiving end of maintenance claims, adopting a methodical and evidence-driven defense is paramount. This approach includes:

- Collecting exhaustive financial documentation covering all assets, liabilities, income streams, and expenditures.
- Utilizing formal legal channels, such as Section 91 applications, to compel disclosure and create an official record.
- Presenting a clear narrative supported by objective evidence to demonstrate either the inability to pay maintenance or to expose the claimant's financial independence.
- Scrutinizing the claimant's financial claims, seeking inconsistencies, and challenging unverifiable liabilities.

- Maintaining transparency and cooperating fully with the court's directives to preserve credibility.

Conversely, for spouses seeking maintenance, the message is clear: full disclosure, honesty, and reasonable expectations are crucial. Courts appreciate genuine cases of financial need but are vigilant against falsehoods or attempts to exploit the system. Establishing and demonstrating inability to maintain oneself or one's children is necessary for fair relief.

It is also important to recognize that maintenance laws are evolving, with courts increasingly relying on modern financial forensics and digital banking records to prevent concealment of income or assets. The days when parties could easily hide wealth or income through shell companies, undisclosed bank accounts, or cash transactions are waning. Courts now employ technology and investigative techniques to uncover the truth, thereby promoting justice.

In conclusion, while maintenance cases often evoke anxiety due to potential financial liabilities, understanding the legal landscape and adopting a strategic, evidence-backed approach can help parties protect their interests effectively. Voluntary departure from the marital home accompanied by unsubstantiated claims of domestic violence does not guarantee maintenance awards. A meticulous presentation of financial facts, combined with procedural rigor such as Section 91 applications, transparency about the claimant's earning capacity, and exposing financial inconsistencies, can lead to favorable judicial outcomes, including the possibility of zero or reduced maintenance.

By respecting the principles of fairness and accountability embedded in family law, and by engaging in honest and thorough financial disclosure, parties can navigate maintenance proceedings with greater confidence and security. The courts' ultimate goal is to ensure equitable support for spouses and children while preventing misuse of legal provisions for undue financial advantage.

Chapter 8

Cross-Border Maintenance: Fighting Fair When You're a Nri

In the realm of matrimonial disputes involving Non-Resident Indians (NRIs), the issue of maintenance payments often presents unique challenges that are not encountered in typical domestic cases. One of the most critical aspects that frequently arises is the question of how to correctly assess the maintenance amount when the husband's income is earned in a foreign currency such as US dollars, British pounds, Swiss francs, or any other stable international currency. This becomes particularly significant because when these foreign earnings are converted directly into Indian rupees at the prevailing exchange rate, the resulting figure often appears substantially inflated in Indian monetary terms. This simplistic conversion can lead to unjust maintenance awards that do not accurately reflect the actual financial position and cost of living of the NRI spouse abroad.

Expense Category	India (Index = 100)	USA	UK	Switzerland	Australia	UAE
Housing	100	250	210	280	220	180
Food	100	160	140	200	150	110
Healthcare	100	350	220	400	250	120
Transportation	100	180	160	220	180	130
Education	100	300	250	350	270	150

This table can show indices for key categories such as housing, food, healthcare, transportation, and education.

The fundamental principle that must guide courts in these cases is the concept of "parity" or "equivalence" of living standards between the country of residence and India. Maintenance is intended to provide for the reasonable needs and expenses of the spouse and dependents, maintaining their standard of living as far as possible. However, this does not mean that the amount of foreign income, when converted into Indian rupees, should be accepted at face value as the basis for maintenance. Instead, the expenses incurred by the NRI in the country of residence must be taken into account to determine the real disposable income available for maintenance purposes. Courts must therefore consider the cost of living, taxation, and other obligatory expenses in the foreign country before fixing maintenance.

The failure to apply this principle often results in courts granting maintenance orders based on inflated rupee amounts, which places an unfair financial burden on the NRI husband. This issue is compounded by the fact that foreign countries typically have a much higher cost of living compared to India. For example, everyday expenses such as housing, healthcare, education, transportation, insurance, and basic necessities tend to be significantly higher in developed countries like the United States, the United Kingdom, Switzerland, or Australia. Additionally, NRIs often face heavy taxation, with income tax rates sometimes reaching 40 to 50 percent or even more, depending on the jurisdiction and income slab.

Moreover, the cost of living in these countries cannot be simply equated with Indian expenses by converting currency. Goods and services available in India at relatively low prices may be prohibitively expensive abroad, even when adjusted for exchange rates. Therefore, maintenance should be calculated after deducting the actual expenses necessary to maintain a similar lifestyle in the foreign country. Courts that overlook these factors may inadvertently cause an inequitable situation where the NRI is compelled to pay maintenance that exceeds their real disposable income, undermining the principle of fairness.

A practical illustration of this can be drawn from a recent case I handled, where my client was residing in Switzerland, earning an income equivalent to around Rs 500,000 per month when converted to Indian rupees. The family court initially fixed a maintenance amount of Rs 100,000 per month based on this converted income figure. This seemed excessive given the cost of living and expenses that my client had to meet in Switzerland. We challenged the order on the ground that the court had failed to consider the parity of the country and the real cost of maintaining a similar standard of living abroad.

Country	Income Tax Rate (%)
India	10-30
USA	20-37
UK	20-45
Switzerland	25-40
Australia	19-45
UAE	0 (No income tax)

Comparing average income tax rates on salaries in India and popular NRI countries, showing how much percentage of income is typically deducted in taxes.

Our argument was twofold: first, the income should be examined net of taxes and obligatory expenses abroad, as a substantial portion of the income was paid in taxes to the Swiss government. Second, the expenses incurred to sustain a lifestyle comparable to that in India, such as higher rent, health insurance, and other essentials, should be factored in. By presenting detailed evidence of these expenses and explaining the economic conditions in Switzerland, we highlighted that the maintenance fixed was not reasonable in the given circumstances.

The court was persuaded by our submissions and granted a stay on the maintenance order after we deposited 50% of the arrears as a show of good faith. Subsequently, the court reconsidered the maintenance amount by applying the parity principle. It was demonstrated that the initial rupee figure was not reflective of the true economic burden on the husband and, consequently, the court agreed to waive off 50% of the arrears and substantially reduce the monthly maintenance obligation. This outcome exemplifies the importance of emphasizing country parity in maintenance cases involving NRIs.

The parity argument is not merely a practical consideration but has strong roots in judicial precedents. Various High Courts and the Supreme Court of India have acknowledged that foreign income cannot be mechanically converted into Indian rupees without regard to the economic realities of the country of residence. Courts have reiterated that maintenance orders must be just and equitable, taking into account the foreign jurisdiction's cost of living and taxation policies. It is therefore a well-accepted legal position that the financial capacity of the NRI should be assessed after deducting taxes and essential living expenses abroad to arrive at a fair maintenance figure.

Another crucial factor that courts must consider is the responsibility that NRIs may have towards their family members residing in India, particularly elderly parents or dependents who rely on their financial support. Such responsibilities reduce the disposable income available for maintenance of the spouse abroad. If an NRI is supporting aged parents or minor children in India, these financial obligations should be factored into the maintenance calculation. Ignoring these dependents while fixing maintenance can distort the actual financial position of the NRI and result in unfairly high awards.

The tax structure abroad often plays a pivotal role in these calculations. For instance, in countries like Switzerland or the United States, income tax rates, social security contributions, and other statutory deductions can reduce the net income by a significant margin. Unlike India, where tax brackets and exemptions differ widely, many foreign countries have flat or progressive tax systems with high rates that materially reduce the disposable income of the earner. Therefore, when courts in India fix maintenance solely based on the gross foreign income converted to rupees, they fail to recognize the economic reality of the NRI's financial situation.

Additionally, the nature of currency fluctuations and exchange rate volatility adds another layer of complexity. Exchange rates between foreign currencies and the Indian rupee can vary substantially over short periods, affecting the perceived value of the NRI's income when converted. Relying strictly on current exchange rates without considering the cost of living adjustment creates an unfair scenario where the maintenance amount could fluctuate unpredictably, destabilizing the financial arrangements. The principle of parity helps stabilize this by focusing on purchasing power and actual expenses rather than mere currency conversion.

In this context, lawyers and litigants must come prepared with detailed documentary evidence about the cost of living abroad, tax obligations, and any dependents supported in India. This evidence can include salary slips, tax returns, bills for rent, utilities, insurance premiums, and proof of financial support to parents or other family members. Expert evidence or affidavits explaining the economic conditions of the foreign country may also strengthen the case. Courts appreciate a methodical approach that quantifies expenses and net income rather than vague assertions, and such an approach enhances the credibility of the parity argument.

To further emphasize the principle, several legal precedents can be cited where courts have upheld the parity argument in NRI maintenance cases. For example, in the case of *Ramesh Chander Kaushal v. Veena Kaushal*, the Supreme Court held that the income of an NRI should not be converted into Indian currency merely at the current exchange rate but must be considered with reference to the cost of living and other financial obligations abroad. Similarly, various High Courts, including the Delhi and Bombay High Courts, have reinforced that maintenance awarded must be equitable and consider the economic status and obligations of the NRI in their country of residence.

The courts have also taken note that maintenance is not intended to penalize the NRI spouse but to provide reasonable financial support. The aim is to preserve fairness by ensuring that the dependent spouse receives sufficient maintenance while not imposing an unrealistic financial burden on the payer. Applying the parity principle achieves this balance by recognizing the economic disparities between countries and ensuring maintenance amounts are grounded in financial realities.

In practice, the success of this argument depends heavily on the quality and depth of the evidence presented. A detailed financial analysis showing the gross foreign income, tax deductions, essential living expenses abroad, and income remitted to India for family support can be persuasive. The litigant should also explain the nature of the currency used for income and the instability or fluctuations that can affect exchange rates. In some cases, evidence of the lifestyle enjoyed by the parties prior to separation may also be relevant to demonstrate the reasonable standard of living to be maintained.

It is also worth noting that courts may consider the nature of the foreign country itself. Developed countries with high living costs justify the parity argument more strongly than countries where living costs are comparable to India. For example, maintenance claims involving NRIs residing in countries like the United States, the United Kingdom, Canada, Australia, or Switzerland generally invoke the parity principle because these countries have much higher cost structures. In contrast, cases involving NRIs living in countries with living expenses closer to India may be evaluated differently.

Apart from maintenance, the parity principle can also be invoked in related matters such as interim relief, child custody expenses, and matrimonial property disputes where the foreign income and economic conditions play a role in determining fair settlements. The holistic approach to foreign income and expenditure fosters a just and balanced adjudication.

In conclusion, the correct approach to fixing maintenance in NRI cases involves more than a simplistic conversion of foreign currency income into Indian rupees. It requires a nuanced assessment of the cost of living in the foreign country, tax liabilities, essential expenses, dependents supported in India, and currency fluctuations. The parity principle serves as a crucial tool for courts to arrive at fair maintenance awards that respect the financial realities of the parties involved. Advocates handling NRI maintenance matters must rigorously argue this principle, supported by detailed evidence and legal precedents, to protect their clients from unjust maintenance demands. Recognizing these complexities and making the court aware of them can significantly influence the outcome, resulting in equitable and just maintenance orders.

Chapter 9

The Endgame: Negotiating Smart Settlements & Closing the Case

In the labyrinth of family law, few battles are as emotionally charged and financially significant as maintenance proceedings. When a husband and wife find themselves entangled in such disputes, the courtroom often becomes a battlefield where every detail of their financial lives is scrutinized. However, beyond the obvious exchanges and visible evidence, the true power often lies in the unseen — the concealed assets, undisclosed incomes, and hidden investments that each party may possess. These hidden facets of their financial affairs, if uncovered and leveraged effectively, can decisively influence the court's decision on maintenance obligations.

Imagine a scenario where a husband, a seemingly modest salaried employee on the surface, is in fact the silent owner of multiple investment portfolios, real estate properties, or even a lucrative side business. On the other side, the wife may have her own income streams, be it through freelancing, undisclosed savings, or inheritances that the husband is unaware of. If either party fails to bring this comprehensive financial picture to light, the court often resorts to standardized maintenance amounts based on the apparent income and needs presented. This standard approach, while providing a baseline, can sometimes lead to unjust outcomes — either overly burdensome or insufficient.

From the vantage point of a legal practitioner defending a husband in maintenance proceedings, the task, therefore, extends beyond mere courtroom argumentation. It is a meticulous investigation into the financial undercurrents that flow beneath the surface. This involves not just reviewing bank statements and tax returns, but proactively searching for hidden accounts, unreported jobs, offshore assets, or undisclosed properties. It also means tapping into the network of professional contacts, financial advisors, and investigators, when necessary, to uncover any signs of financial obfuscation.

Why is this level of detail so critical? Because courts in India, while sympathetic to the genuine needs of the wife and children, fundamentally base their orders on evidence before them. The Supreme Court and various High Courts have repeatedly emphasized that maintenance must be fair, just, and reasonable, reflecting the husband's ability to pay as well as the wife's genuine requirements. If your client's financial might is grossly underestimated by the court due to lack of evidence, the maintenance amount imposed may become unnecessarily high. Conversely, revealing the wife's own financial strength could reduce the perceived necessity of maintenance, thereby lowering or even nullifying the claim.

This principle of uncovering the truth is illustrated in several landmark judgments. For instance, courts have held that the husband's actual income and lifestyle must be accounted for, including perks, allowances, or any benefits that may not be immediately obvious. On the flip side, courts have also noted that the wife is expected to make reasonable efforts to become self-reliant if she is capable of working or has sources of income. Such nuances underscore the importance of a thorough financial assessment.

To put this into perspective, consider a case where the husband initially claimed a modest salary, but evidence revealed his ownership of multiple properties rented out at substantial monthly income. The revelation led to a revision of maintenance orders, increasing the husband's liability significantly. In contrast, another case saw a wife claiming a large maintenance amount based on her supposed lack of income, only for the defense to produce evidence of her independent consultancy work, which substantially reduced the court's award. These cases serve as practical lessons in the strategic significance of financial transparency.

While engaging in these proceedings, it is equally important to maintain a clear head and avoid the pitfalls of ego and emotional escalation. Maintenance disputes are deeply personal and often intertwined with feelings of betrayal, anger, or disappointment. Whether the wife left the matrimonial home due to extramarital affairs, temperamental differences, or other faults, the courts generally prioritize the welfare of the wife and children over marital discord. The Indian judiciary has consistently maintained that maintenance is a right of the wife and children, not a punishment for the husband. Therefore, even in cases where fault is apparent, maintenance is usually granted to ensure the sustenance and dignity of the dependents.

Understanding this legal philosophy is crucial for strategizing defense. Rather than contesting maintenance on moral grounds or blame, it is more pragmatic to assess realistically what maintenance amount the court is likely to impose based on the husband's true financial position and the wife's needs. This assessment allows for better decision-making on whether to pursue prolonged litigation or consider alternative dispute resolution.

Speaking of alternatives, settlements in maintenance cases often provide the most efficient and amicable resolution. A negotiated settlement, especially if it closely approximates the maintenance arrears that would otherwise be payable, can save the parties significant time, expense, and emotional strain. Furthermore, a well-drafted settlement can also bring closure to related matrimonial disputes, including pending divorce proceedings, thus allowing both parties to move forward without the lingering uncertainty of ongoing litigation.

Settlements carry their own strategic value. For the husband, they can cap financial exposure and avoid unpredictable court decisions. For the wife, they provide immediate relief and a guaranteed sum without the delays and uncertainties of trial. Of course, the settlement must be carefully evaluated to ensure fairness and compliance with legal standards, as courts do have the power to reject settlements that appear unconscionable or detrimental to the welfare of the children.

To illustrate, a client once faced a prolonged maintenance dispute where the wife demanded a large monthly sum. After detailed financial discovery and honest assessment, it became clear that the court would likely impose a slightly lower amount, but with considerable delay and legal costs. The client opted to offer a lump sum settlement covering maintenance arrears and future payments for a defined period. The wife accepted, and the dispute was resolved swiftly, saving both parties months of litigation and tens of thousands in legal fees.

Navigating maintenance cases also demands attention to procedural nuances and timelines. Interim maintenance applications, often filed at the early stages of a case, set the tone for subsequent proceedings. Courts typically grant interim maintenance based on prima facie assessment of the husband's ability and the wife's immediate needs. Therefore, having financial evidence ready even at this stage can influence the interim orders significantly. Subsequent hearings focus on final maintenance, where a more detailed inquiry is conducted.

One cannot underestimate the importance of documentation in these cases. Income tax returns, salary slips, bank statements, property papers, and investment certificates form the backbone of any financial disclosure. Any gaps or inconsistencies can weaken the defense's position or provide grounds for the court to suspect concealment. Conversely, comprehensive and transparent documentation enhances credibility and often garners judicial favor.

In parallel, an awareness of relevant statutes and judicial precedents enriches the defense strategy. The Maintenance and Welfare of Parents and Senior Citizens Act, 2007, the Hindu Adoption and Maintenance Act, 1956, and the Code of Criminal Procedure (Section 125) provide statutory frameworks for maintenance claims. Landmark Supreme Court rulings have clarified aspects such as the criteria for maintenance, the need for self-sufficiency by the wife, and the limits of judicial discretion.

For example, the Supreme Court in the landmark case of *Mohd. Ahmed Khan v. Shah Bano Begum* (1985) laid down that maintenance must be just and reasonable, reflecting both the husband's financial capacity and the wife's standard of living during the marriage. This principle continues to guide courts in ensuring maintenance amounts that neither impoverish the husband nor leave the wife destitute.

In today's digital age, financial transparency extends beyond traditional documents. Bank accounts, investments, and even cryptocurrency wallets can be scrutinized if there is suspicion of concealment. This makes it essential for the defending party's legal team to be conversant with modern investigative techniques and to work closely with forensic accountants when needed.

However, despite all these complexities, one fact remains clear: the ultimate aim of maintenance law is to uphold the dignity and welfare of those dependent on support. It is not meant to be punitive, but protective. Recognizing this balance and strategizing accordingly is the hallmark of effective legal representation in maintenance matters.

As you journey through this book, you will find detailed chapters explaining these principles with case studies, procedural checklists, and strategic guidance. Each page is designed to equip you with a comprehensive understanding of how maintenance proceedings unfold in India, the pitfalls to avoid, and the best practices for crafting a robust defense.

Should you encounter questions or challenges along the way, remember that you are not alone. The law is complex, but so is the community of legal professionals dedicated to mastering it. I invite you to reach out to me directly via email for personalized guidance or to join our dynamic WhatsApp community group. This group is a vibrant platform where lawyers and professionals share insights, discuss evolving jurisprudence, and support one another through the intricacies of maintenance law.

Whether you are a practicing advocate, a law student, or an individual navigating a maintenance case, this community offers an invaluable resource. Here, collective wisdom meets practical experience, and every member is empowered to defend rights and protect interests more effectively.

Together, let us foster a spirit of collaboration and mutual assistance. Maintenance proceedings need not be a journey marked by conflict and confusion. With the right knowledge, tools, and support network, you can navigate these legal waters with confidence and efficacy, securing fair outcomes for all parties involved.

This book is your companion, your guide, and your strategy manual. Let us embark on this journey together, turning challenges into opportunities and legal complexities into clear, actionable steps.

Chapter 10

Evolution of Maintenance Jurisprudence in India: From *Rupali Gupta v. Rajat Gupta* to *Rajnesh v. Neha*

The development of maintenance law in India reflects the dynamic interplay between statutory provisions, social norms, and judicial interpretation. Maintenance, in its essence, is a measure to prevent destitution and ensure a degree of financial security to dependent spouses and children following marital breakdown or desertion. Over the years, the courts have played a vital role in interpreting the scope, nature, and enforceability of maintenance obligations. Among the important milestones in this evolution are the judgments in *Rupali Gupta v. Rajat Gupta* and *Rajnesh v. Neha*, which together trace the shift in maintenance jurisprudence from a substantive recognition of entitlement to a procedural consolidation and standardization of the law.

Historically, the law relating to maintenance was governed by multiple enactments depending on the personal laws applicable to the parties. These include Section 125 of the Code of Criminal Procedure, 1973, which is a secular and summary remedy; Section 24 and 25 of the Hindu Marriage Act, 1955, dealing with interim and permanent alimony; Section 18 of the Hindu Adoptions and Maintenance Act, 1956; and Section 20 of the Protection of Women from Domestic Violence Act, 2005, among others. The multiplicity of statutes led to overlapping claims, procedural confusion, and at times, conflicting orders from different forums. In this context, the interpretation of the right to maintenance, the determination of quantum, and the approach to adjudication evolved significantly through judicial intervention.

In *Rupali Gupta v. Rajat Gupta*, decided by the Delhi High Court in 2009, the court dealt with a significant issue concerning the denial of interim maintenance under Section 24 of the Hindu Marriage Act to an educated wife on the ground that she was capable of earning. The wife in this case had filed an application seeking maintenance during the pendency of the matrimonial litigation. The trial court rejected the claim, reasoning that the wife was an educated woman with professional qualifications and hence was not entitled to interim maintenance. The matter came before the High Court in appeal.

Justice S. Ravindra Bhat, delivering the judgment, held that the denial of maintenance merely on the ground of educational qualification or potential earning capacity was legally unsustainable. The court observed that an estranged wife cannot be compelled to work merely because she is educated. The right to maintenance, particularly under Section 24, must be viewed in the light of the standard of living enjoyed during marriage and the financial disparity between the spouses. The court emphasized that the purpose of maintenance is to ensure that the economically weaker spouse is not rendered destitute or placed at a severe disadvantage during the litigation.

This ruling was a significant development as it clarified that the right to maintenance is not contingent on the wife's actual employment but rather on her financial needs and the economic imbalance resulting from separation. It moved away from a rigid assessment based on theoretical earning potential and laid down a more equitable standard based on real-life circumstances. The court recognized the non-financial contributions of a spouse to the marriage and the value of unpaid domestic labor, thus providing a broader understanding of dependency and entitlement.

However, while the *Rupali Gupta* judgment strengthened the substantive right of spouses to claim maintenance, especially women, it did not address the larger procedural and systemic issues plaguing maintenance litigation. Across the country, maintenance cases were marred by delays, inconsistent orders, evasion of disclosure by parties, and misuse of parallel proceedings under multiple enactments. The lack of uniform criteria for income assessment and the absence of enforcement mechanisms further compounded the problem.

It was in response to these widespread concerns that the Supreme Court in *Rajnesh v. Neha*, decided in November 2020, undertook a comprehensive reformulation of the procedural framework governing maintenance proceedings. The case arose out of a maintenance dispute under Section 125 of the Criminal Procedure Code. The respondent-wife, Neha, filed an application for maintenance for herself and her minor son, alleging desertion and non-support by her husband, Rajnesh. The litigation saw protracted proceedings, non-compliance with interim orders, and multiple legal actions in different forums. Recognizing the systemic malaise, the Supreme Court, instead of limiting its inquiry to the individual facts of the case, proceeded to lay down detailed guidelines aimed at overhauling the conduct of maintenance litigation across the country.

The Supreme Court in *Rajnesh v. Neha* addressed five key areas: standardization of financial disclosures, overlapping jurisdiction under various maintenance laws, the date from which maintenance should be granted, enforcement of maintenance orders, and judicial training. First and foremost, the court made it mandatory for both parties to file a detailed affidavit of assets, income, expenditure, and liabilities at the initial stage of the proceedings. The court annexed two formats of affidavits—one for salaried individuals and the other for self-employed or income-variable persons. These affidavits require disclosure of income tax returns, bank account details, property documents, loan liabilities, credit card statements, lifestyle indicators, and expenditures. The objective was to ensure transparency, discourage suppression of income, and enable the court to arrive at a fair assessment of the financial status of the parties.

This direction addressed a major lacuna in maintenance adjudication. Until this judgment, courts had no standardized method of evaluating the income and living standards of the parties. Litigants often manipulated or suppressed financial information to either inflate claims or minimize liability. The affidavit mechanism introduced by the Supreme Court created a uniform evidentiary base, allowing judges to make informed decisions and reducing the scope for ambiguity and arbitrariness.

Secondly, the Supreme Court addressed the issue of multiplicity of proceedings. It noted that litigants frequently filed parallel claims under Section 125 CrPC, the Hindu Marriage Act, and the Domestic Violence Act, resulting in conflicting maintenance awards. The court directed that parties must disclose all existing proceedings and maintenance orders to the court where a new claim is filed. The courts were instructed to avoid granting multiple or overlapping reliefs and instead adjust maintenance amounts awarded under different statutes. This directive was aimed at preventing forum shopping, abuse of process, and unnecessary harassment of the respondent spouse.

Thirdly, the Supreme Court settled the contentious issue regarding the date from which maintenance should be awarded. Courts across jurisdictions were divided on whether maintenance should be granted from the date of application or the date of order. The Supreme Court ruled that, as a general rule, maintenance should be awarded from the date of filing of the application unless there are compelling reasons to hold otherwise. This clarification provided much-needed certainty and protected the claimant spouse from prolonged financial insecurity during the pendency of litigation.

Fourthly, the court emphasized the importance of enforcement of maintenance orders. It observed that delayed or non-payment of maintenance defeats the very object of the law and leaves the claimant spouse and children vulnerable. The court directed that trial courts must adopt strict measures to ensure compliance, including the use of civil detention, attachment of property, and other coercive mechanisms provided under the law. It also noted that non-compliance could lead to consequences such as striking off the defense of the defaulter in appropriate cases.

Finally, the Supreme Court underscored the need for judicial training and standardization of practice. It directed that its guidelines be circulated to all High Courts and through them to the subordinate judiciary. Family courts and magistrates were to be trained to ensure consistent application of the judgment and to adopt a sensitive and realistic approach to maintenance disputes. The judgment acknowledged that the quality of maintenance adjudication is deeply linked to the competence and awareness of the adjudicating authority.

Taken together, the directives issued in *Rajnesh v. Neha* marked a paradigm shift in maintenance jurisprudence. Unlike earlier decisions which focused primarily on the substantive right to claim maintenance, *Rajnesh v. Neha* sought to institutionalize procedural fairness, standardize judicial practice, and ensure effective enforcement. It recognized that without a robust procedural framework, even the most progressive interpretation of the law remains ineffective in practice.

The evolution from *Rupali Gupta* to *Rajnesh v. Neha* thus captures the broader trajectory of maintenance law in India. In *Rupali Gupta*, the court focused on the substantive right of a spouse—particularly the wife—to receive maintenance based on actual dependence and standard of living, rather than notional earning capacity. The court recognized that unpaid domestic labor and emotional support in a marriage are valuable contributions and that the financial dependence of a wife cannot be negated solely on the basis of her education. This judgment helped shift the discourse from a patriarchal understanding of dependency to a more holistic view of economic justice within marriage.

In contrast, *Rajnesh v. Neha* sought to address the structural weaknesses in the implementation of maintenance laws. It laid down the foundation for a more predictable, transparent, and enforceable model of maintenance adjudication. While the earlier jurisprudence acknowledged the need for maintenance as a moral and legal obligation, *Rajnesh v. Neha* provided the administrative tools and procedural safeguards necessary to actualize that obligation effectively and uniformly across the legal system.

This journey also reflects the evolving role of the judiciary in family law matters—from a primarily adjudicatory function to an increasingly policy-oriented role. Courts have stepped in not merely to interpret statutory provisions but to fill legislative gaps, prescribe uniform formats, and guide institutional practices. This is particularly significant in a country like India where personal laws are diverse and legislative reform is often slow.

In conclusion, the transition from *Rupali Gupta* to *Rajnesh v. Neha* signifies the maturation of Indian maintenance jurisprudence. It represents a shift from the recognition of rights in theory to their enforcement in practice. The courts have moved from viewing maintenance as a mere interim relief to treating it as a comprehensive legal entitlement backed by procedural safeguards. This evolution is a testament to the judiciary's responsiveness to the lived realities of matrimonial disputes and its commitment to ensuring substantive and procedural justice for all stakeholders in a marriage. The combined impact of these judgments has set the foundation for a more equitable and efficient system of matrimonial dispute resolution, rooted in constitutional values and social welfare principles.

Chapter 11

The Landmark of Maintenance Laws : Rajnesh v. Neha

The landmark Supreme Court judgment in *Rajnesh v. Neha*, decided on 4th November 2020, has brought a transformative shift in the approach towards maintenance proceedings in India. The decision, rendered by a bench comprising Justice Indu Malhotra and Justice R. Subhash Reddy, was delivered in the backdrop of increasing delays, multiplicity of proceedings, and inconsistent practices in awarding maintenance under different statutes such as Section 125 of the Criminal Procedure Code, 1973, the Hindu Marriage Act, 1955, and the Protection of Women from Domestic Violence Act, 2005. The Court undertook the task of harmonizing these provisions and laying down uniform guidelines that would apply across various forums dealing with maintenance cases.

The factual matrix of the case involved a maintenance dispute between a wife, Neha, and her estranged husband, Rajnesh. The wife had filed an application under Section

125 CrPC seeking maintenance for herself and their minor son. Despite interim orders passed by the courts, there was prolonged litigation, delayed payments, and non-compliance by the husband. The Supreme Court, upon hearing the matter, noted that maintenance litigation is often used as a tool of harassment, that procedural inconsistencies result in hardship to the claimant spouse and children, and that there is a lack of uniformity in how different courts assess the financial capabilities of the parties involved.

Addressing these issues, the Supreme Court issued comprehensive directions, setting out a framework to streamline maintenance proceedings in all courts across the country. One of the most significant contributions of the judgment was the introduction of mandatory filing of detailed affidavits of disclosure of income, assets, expenditure, and liabilities by both parties. These affidavits were made obligatory at the very first stage of the proceedings, so that the court could fairly assess the financial status of the parties while granting interim or final maintenance. The Court annexed two formats—one for salaried individuals and one for self-employed or business persons—which now form the standard disclosure tool in most maintenance cases. These affidavits require parties to disclose income tax returns, bank account details, ownership of movable and immovable properties, loans, credit card statements, and even lifestyle indicators such as number of vehicles owned or foreign travel undertaken. The objective was to curb suppression of income, reduce the scope of false claims, and bring transparency to the process.

The Court also took note of the overlapping jurisdiction of various forums. It observed that it had become common for spouses to simultaneously file maintenance applications under multiple statutes, leading to conflicting decisions, forum shopping, and multiplicity of litigation. To address this, the Court directed that in all maintenance proceedings, the parties must mandatorily disclose the pendency or outcome of any other maintenance proceedings under different laws. The court concerned must then either consolidate or adjust the maintenance awarded under different provisions to avoid duplication. The ruling further clarified that parties are not entitled to claim separate or additional maintenance under each statute unless it has been specifically justified and adjudicated upon.

On the issue of the starting point for awarding maintenance, the Court settled the legal position by holding that, in general, maintenance should be granted from the date of filing of the application, unless there are exceptional circumstances warranting a different approach. This finding resolved a previously unsettled question, where some courts awarded maintenance from the date of order and others from the date of application, resulting in inconsistent relief to the claimants. The judgment also emphasized that delays in payment of maintenance should not be tolerated and that courts must ensure that the orders are enforced strictly. In cases of willful non-compliance, the court is empowered to adopt coercive measures such as issuance of warrants, civil detention, or attachment of property.

The Supreme Court also laid down principles for granting permanent alimony under Section 25 of the Hindu Marriage Act. It stated that while determining the quantum of permanent alimony, the courts must take into consideration a range of factors including the standard of living during marriage, the duration of the marriage, the financial and non-financial contribution of the claimant spouse, age, health, and the capacity to earn. The Court cautioned against adopting a mechanical or arbitrary approach and stressed that the determination should be just, equitable, and realistic.

In addition to procedural reforms, the Court emphasized the importance of judicial discipline and training. It directed that the judgment be circulated to all High Courts for onward transmission to family courts, magistrates, and trial courts across the country. The aim was to ensure that the guidelines are uniformly implemented and that maintenance proceedings are not reduced to lengthy, adversarial battles. The Court also noted the need for periodic judicial training and sensitization of presiding officers, especially in family courts, to ensure that the purpose of maintenance law is achieved in both letter and spirit.

From a legal and policy standpoint, *Rajnesh v. Neha* represents a critical evolution in maintenance jurisprudence. Before this decision, maintenance proceedings were often marked by arbitrary orders, lack of proper financial assessment, and prolonged procedural delays. By introducing the affidavit of assets and liabilities and streamlining overlapping jurisdiction, the

Supreme Court brought in a uniform and transparent mechanism that can be relied upon across statutes and forums. The affidavit format not only enables the courts to assess income and expenditure accurately, but also ensures accountability of both parties. The ruling thus balances the rights of the wife and children to receive timely maintenance with the rights of the husband to fair adjudication, especially in cases where exaggerated or fraudulent claims may be made.

The judgment further marked a significant shift from discretion-based adjudication to standardized and principle-based decision-making. It recognized the socio-economic realities faced by deserted or estranged spouses, especially women, who often lack access to financial resources or legal support. At the same time, it took into account the need to protect individuals from abuse of process or harassment through multiple proceedings. The judgment lays a foundation for future reforms, especially in integrating digital affidavits, improving enforcement mechanisms, and introducing statutory amendments for procedural uniformity.

However, the practical implementation of the *Rajnesh v. Neha* guidelines remains a challenge. While many High Courts have adopted and circulated the affidavit formats, compliance at the trial court level is still inconsistent. Courts often delay the enforcement of affidavit filing, or grant repeated adjournments, thereby diluting the effectiveness of the judgment. Additionally, while the Court made observations about penalizing false or misleading affidavits, there is limited data on whether courts have taken serious action in such cases. Despite these concerns, the judgment is a vital step forward in building a fairer and more efficient system for adjudicating maintenance claims.

In conclusion, *Rajnesh v. Neha* is a landmark decision that has redefined the procedural and substantive contours of maintenance litigation in India. It has brought about a much-needed structural reform by introducing a transparent mechanism for financial disclosure, harmonizing maintenance jurisprudence across statutes, and strengthening the enforcement of maintenance orders. The judgment balances gender justice with legal prudence and curbs the misuse of maintenance laws while upholding their welfare objective. It has also shifted the focus of courts from discretionary decision-making to evidence-based and structured adjudication. As maintenance litigation continues to be one of the most litigated areas in family law, the judgment in *Rajnesh v. Neha* offers a guiding framework that courts, lawyers, and litigants can uniformly rely upon. It represents not just a judicial pronouncement but a judicial policy reform—one that advances access to justice, procedural efficiency, and fairness in matrimonial disputes.